The Little Margarita Cocktail Recipe Book

The Little Margarita Cocktail Recipe Book

MYTHIC MIXOLOGY
Cocktail Recipes for Nerds

Cocktail recipes curated for enthusiasts and nerds alike. Drawing inspiration from themes of science fiction, enchanting realms of fantasy, rich tapestries of literature, and the intricate annals of world histories.

The Little Margarita

COCKTAIL RECIPE BOOK

Table of Contents

Introduction

Margaritas are more than just a cocktail; they are an experience, a tradition, and a celebration in a glass. With their perfect balance of sweet, sour, salty, and bitter, margaritas have secured a beloved spot in the hearts of cocktail enthusiasts around the world. This book is a tribute to the endless possibilities that the margarita offers, showcasing a plethora of flavor variations that elevate this classic drink to new and exciting heights. Whether you are a seasoned mixologist or a home bartender, this collection of recipes is designed to inspire creativity and bring joy to your margarita-making adventures.

The origins of the margarita are shrouded in mystery, with several colorful stories vying for the title of the true creation tale. Some say it was invented in the late 1930s by a Mexican bartender for a beautiful showgirl named Marjorie King who was allergic to all spirits except tequila. Others claim it was crafted by Texas socialite Margarita Sames during a party at her vacation home in Acapulco. Regardless of its true beginnings, the margarita quickly gained popularity and became a symbol of good times and relaxation.

At its core, a margarita is a simple combination of tequila, lime juice, and triple sec. However, this simplicity is what makes it such a versatile canvas for experimentation. The balance of these three ingredients creates a harmonious blend that can be easily adapted to include a wide variety of flavors and ingredients. From the classic lime margarita to exotic fruit blends, spicy infusions, and herbal concoctions, the possibilities are truly endless.

One of the key elements of a great margarita is the quality of the ingredients. Tequila, the star of the show, should be chosen with care. A good quality blanco tequila offers a clean and crisp flavor, while a reposado or añejo tequila can add depth and complexity with its aged characteristics. Freshly squeezed lime juice is essential, as it provides the bright, tangy acidity that balances the sweetness of the triple sec. Speaking of triple sec, opting for a high-quality orange liqueur, such as Cointreau or Grand Marnier, can make a noticeable difference in the overall taste of your margarita.

Salt is another important component, traditionally used to rim the glass. The salt enhances the flavors and provides a delightful contrast to the sweet and sour elements of the drink. Experimenting with different types of salt, such as sea salt, smoked salt, or flavored salts, can add an interesting twist to your margarita. For those who prefer a sweeter touch, sugar rims or even crushed cookies can be a fun alternative.

As we delve into the world of margarita variations, it's important to remember that the joy of making margaritas lies in the creativity and experimentation. This book is filled with recipes that range from traditional to innovative, each one designed to inspire you to try new combinations and find your personal favorites. Whether you're looking for a refreshing summertime sipper, a bold and spicy concoction, or a dessert-like treat, you'll find a recipe that suits your mood and occasion.

Fruit margaritas are a delightful way to introduce new flavors and add a burst of color to your cocktail. Fresh, ripe fruits such as strawberries, mangoes, pineapples, and raspberries can be blended into the drink or used as a garnish. Tropical fruits like passion fruit, guava, and kiwi offer an exotic twist, transporting your taste buds to a sunny paradise. For a more unique flavor profile, try incorporating unusual fruits like dragon fruit, lychee, or tamarind. Each fruit brings its own distinct character, sweetness, and acidity, allowing you to create a truly customized margarita experience.

Herbs and spices can also play a significant role in elevating your margarita game. Fresh herbs like mint, basil, cilantro, and rosemary can be muddled into the drink or used as a garnish to add an aromatic, refreshing element. Spices such as chili powder, cayenne pepper, or smoked paprika can introduce a hint of heat, balancing the sweetness and adding a bold kick. Infusing your tequila with spices or herbs is another way to impart unique flavors. Imagine a jalapeño-infused tequila for a spicy margarita, or a lavender-infused tequila for a floral, aromatic twist. The possibilities are limited only by your imagination.

The margarita's versatility also extends to the choice of sweeteners. While simple syrup is a common choice, you can experiment with other sweeteners like agave nectar, honey, or maple syrup. Each sweetener brings its own flavor profile and can complement different fruits and spices. For a more complex sweetness, try using flavored syrups such as ginger syrup, hibiscus syrup, or even homemade fruit syrups. These additions not only enhance the flavor but also add depth and complexity to your margarita.

For those who enjoy a bit of fizz in their drinks, adding a splash of soda water, sparkling wine, or even flavored soda can add a delightful effervescence to your margarita. This addition can lighten the drink and provide a refreshing, bubbly texture that is perfect for celebrations and special occasions. Imagine a sparkling grapefruit margarita with a hint of rosemary, or a champagne mango margarita with a touch of mint. These sparkling variations are sure to impress and add a festive touch to any gathering.

Another exciting aspect of margaritas is the ability to play with different textures. While a classic margarita on the rocks offers a crisp and refreshing experience, a blended margarita provides a smooth, slushy texture that is perfect for hot summer days. Converting a margarita on the rocks to a blended version is a simple process that can easily be done with any recipe. To make this transformation, take the same ingredients used for the on-the-rocks version and combine them in a blender with a generous amount of ice. Blend until smooth, adjusting the ice to achieve your desired consistency. This method ensures that the flavor profile remains consistent while offering the unique texture and cooling effect of a blended drink.

In addition to the endless flavor combinations, the presentation of your margarita can also make a significant impact. The glassware you choose, the garnishes you add, and the way you rim the glass all contribute to the overall experience. A classic margarita glass is always a great choice, but don't be afraid to mix things up with different types of glassware. Highball glasses, rocks glasses, and even mason jars can add a fun and casual touch to your presentation. The key is to choose a glass that complements the style of your margarita and enhances the drinking experience.

Garnishes are a fantastic way to add visual appeal and additional flavors to your margarita. Traditional garnishes like lime wheels, salt rims, and fresh herbs are always a hit, but you can also get creative with your choices. Consider adding edible flowers, fresh fruit slices, or even candy to your garnishes. A sprig of rosemary, a slice of jalapeño, or a twist of citrus peel can add a touch of elegance and intrigue. For a more playful approach, try rimming your glass with flavored salts, sugars, or even crushed cookies.

The joy of making margaritas lies in the process of experimentation and discovery. Each recipe in this book is designed to be a starting point, encouraging you to explore new flavors and techniques. Don't be afraid to adjust the ingredients and proportions to suit your taste. If you prefer a sweeter margarita, add a bit more syrup or fruit puree. If you like it more tart, increase the amount of lime juice. The beauty of margaritas is their adaptability, allowing you to create a drink that is perfectly tailored to your preferences.

Hosting a margarita party is a fantastic way to share your love of this versatile cocktail with friends and family. Set up a margarita bar with a variety of ingredients and let your guests customize their own drinks. Provide different types of tequilas, citrus juices, sweeteners, and garnishes, and encourage everyone to experiment with their own unique combinations. This interactive approach not only makes for a fun and engaging event but also allows everyone to discover their perfect margarita.

As you embark on this margarita journey, remember that the most important ingredient is joy. The joy of experimenting with new flavors, the joy of sharing your creations with others, and the joy of savoring a delicious, refreshing cocktail. Whether you're sipping a classic lime margarita on the rocks or enjoying a tropical mango margarita blended to perfection, each sip is a celebration of creativity and craftsmanship.

In the pages that follow, you'll find a diverse collection of margarita recipes that showcase the endless possibilities of this beloved cocktail. From traditional favorites to innovative new twists, each recipe is designed to inspire and delight. Whether you're a purist who loves the simplicity of a classic margarita or an adventurous mixologist eager to explore new flavors, there is something here for everyone. So, grab your shaker, your blender, and your favorite tequila, and get ready to embark on a delicious and exciting margarita adventure.

Cheers to exploring the wonderful world of margaritas, to discovering new and exciting flavors, and to creating your own signature cocktails. May each recipe bring you joy, inspire your creativity, and enhance your appreciation for this timeless and versatile drink. Here's to the perfect margarita and to the endless possibilities that await in every glass.

Blended, Rocks, Etc.

They say there are two kinds of people in this world: those who prefer their margaritas blended and those who like them on the rocks. It's a debate as old as time, or at least as old as the first margarita mixer. Whether you enjoy the crisp, clear flavors of a margarita on the rocks or the frosty, smooth texture of a blended margarita, there's no wrong way to enjoy this beloved cocktail. Each style has its own unique charm and appeal, making margaritas a versatile favorite for any occasion. The margaritas in this book are mostly designed to be served on the rocks, but don't worry, converting them to blended versions is simple and straightforward.

A margarita on the rocks is the epitome of classic elegance. It allows each ingredient to shine through distinctly, offering a refreshing balance of tequila, citrus, and sweetness. The ice cools the drink without overly diluting it, so every sip provides a burst of clean, unadulterated flavor. You can taste the sharpness of the lime, the warmth of the tequila, and the subtle sweetness of the triple sec. This version is perfect for those who appreciate the complexity and clarity of each component, creating a refined drinking experience that is both refreshing and invigorating.

On the other hand, a blended margarita offers a different kind of delight. By integrating all the ingredients into a smooth, slushy mixture, the blended margarita becomes a cohesive and indulgent treat. The crushed ice creates a frosty texture that is particularly enjoyable on a hot day, offering a cooling sensation that is both satisfying and fun. Blended margaritas tend to be slightly more diluted, but this can be easily adjusted by controlling the amount of ice used. The result is a drink that feels more like a dessert, with the flavors melding together into a harmonious whole.

Converting a margarita on the rocks to a blended version is a simple process that can easily be done with any recipe. To make this transformation, take the same ingredients used for the on-the-rocks version and combine them in a blender with a generous amount of ice. Blend until smooth, adjusting the ice to achieve your desired consistency. This method ensures that the flavor profile remains consistent while offering the unique texture and cooling effect of a blended drink.

One of the joys of making margaritas is the ability to experiment with different ingredients and flavors. The recipes in this book are designed to be versatile, encouraging you to play around and find what suits your taste best. For instance, if a recipe calls for homemade ginger syrup but you're short on time or ingredients, you can easily substitute ginger ale or ginger beer. These alternatives provide the desired ginger flavor and add a bit of fizz, enhancing the overall experience.

Similarly, if a recipe includes fresh pineapple puree and you don't have any on hand, juice from canned pineapple can be an excellent substitute. The canned juice offers a slightly sweeter note and can be used just as effectively in your margarita. The key to a great margarita lies in balancing the flavors of the tequila, citrus, and any additional ingredients. Whether on the rocks or blended, the goal is to create a drink that is refreshing, flavorful, and enjoyable.

Feel free to get creative with your margaritas. Fresh fruits, different sweeteners, and various herbs can all be incorporated to create your unique twist on the classic cocktail. Adding fresh berries, such as strawberries, raspberries, or blackberries, can provide a burst of color and flavor, making your margarita both visually appealing and delicious. Fresh herbs like mint, basil, or cilantro can add a refreshing aromatic note, while spices like chili powder or cayenne pepper can introduce a hint of heat, balancing the sweetness and adding a bold kick.

For those who enjoy a bit of fizz, consider adding a splash of sparkling water, club soda, or even champagne to your margarita. This addition can lighten the drink and provide a refreshing, bubbly texture that is perfect for celebrations and special occasions. Imagine a sparkling grapefruit margarita with a touch of rosemary, or a champagne mango margarita with a hint of mint. These sparkling variations are sure to impress and add a festive touch to any gathering.

Another exciting aspect of margaritas is the ability to play with different textures. While a classic margarita on the rocks offers a crisp and refreshing experience, a blended margarita provides a smooth, slushy texture that is perfect for hot summer days. Converting a margarita on the rocks to a blended version is a simple process that can easily be done with any recipe. To make this transformation, take the same ingredients used for the on-the-rocks version and combine them in a blender with a generous amount of ice. Blend until smooth, adjusting the ice to achieve your desired consistency. This method ensures that the flavor profile remains consistent while offering the unique texture and cooling effect of a blended drink.

In addition to the endless flavor combinations, the presentation of your margarita can also make a significant impact. The glassware you choose, the garnishes you add, and the way you rim the glass all contribute to the overall experience. A classic margarita glass is always a great choice, but don't be afraid to mix things up with different types of glassware. Highball glasses, rocks glasses, and even mason jars can add a fun and casual touch to your presentation. The key is to choose a glass that complements the style of your margarita and enhances the drinking experience.

Garnishes are a fantastic way to add visual appeal and additional flavors to your margarita. Traditional garnishes like lime wheels, salt rims, and fresh herbs are always a hit, but you can also get creative with your choices. Consider adding edible flowers, fresh fruit slices, or even candy to your garnishes. A sprig of rosemary, a slice of jalapeño, or a twist of citrus peel can add a touch of elegance and intrigue. For a more playful approach, try rimming your glass with flavored salts, sugars, or even crushed cookies.

The joy of making margaritas lies in the process of experimentation and discovery. Each recipe in this book is designed to be a starting point, encouraging you to explore new flavors and techniques. Don't be afraid to adjust the ingredients and proportions to suit your taste. If you prefer a sweeter margarita, add a bit more syrup or fruit puree. If you like it more tart, increase the amount of lime juice. The beauty of margaritas is their adaptability, allowing you to create a drink that is perfectly tailored to your preferences.

So whether you're a fan of the crisp, distinct flavors of a margarita on the rocks or the smooth, integrated experience of a blended margarita, this book has something for everyone. Gather your ingredients, unleash your creativity, and enjoy the delightful journey of crafting the ultimate margarita. Cheers to the endless possibilities and the joy of discovering your perfect margarita.

Recipes

Classic Margarita

- ➤ 2 oz tequila
- ➤ 1 oz lime juice, freshly squeezed
- ➤ 1/2 oz triple sec
- ➤ Ice cubes
- ➤ Salt for rimming the glass
- ➤ Lime wedge for garnish

Salt the Rim: Rub a lime wedge around the rim of a margarita glass and dip the rim in salt.

Combine Ingredients: In a shaker, combine the tequila, lime juice, and Cointreau.

Add Ice: Fill the shaker with ice, covering the liquid.

Shake Vigorously: Shake until the outside of the shaker feels cold, about 15 seconds.

Strain: Strain the cocktail into the prepared glass filled with fresh ice.

Garnish: Add a lime wedge on the rim of the glass.

Serve: Serve immediately and enjoy the refreshing and iconic flavors of your Classic Margarita.

Almond Margarita

- 2 oz tequila
- 1 oz lime juice, freshly squeezed
- 1/2 oz Amaretto
- 1/2 oz simple syrup
- Ice cubes
- Salt for rimming the glass
- Lime wedge and a few toasted almonds for garnish

Salt the Rim: Rub a lime wedge around the rim of a margarita glass and dip the rim in salt.

Combine Ingredients: In a cocktail shaker, combine the tequila, lime juice, almond liqueur, and simple syrup.

Add Ice: Fill the shaker with ice cubes.

Shake Vigorously: Shake well until the mixture is thoroughly chilled.

Strain: Strain the cocktail into the prepared glass filled with fresh ice.

Garnish: Decorate with a lime wedge on the rim and sprinkle a few toasted almonds on top.

Serve: Serve immediately and savor the smooth, nutty flavors of your Almond Margarita.

Ancho Chile Margarita

- 2 oz tequila
- 1 oz lime juice, freshly squeezed
- 1/2 oz triple sec
- 1/2 oz ancho chile liqueur
- 1/4 oz simple syrup
- Ice cubes
- Salt and chili powder for rimming the glass
- Lime wedge for garnish

Prepare the Rim: Mix a little salt with chili powder. Rub a lime wedge around the rim of a margarita glass and dip it into the salt-chili mixture.

Combine Ingredients: In a cocktail shaker, combine the tequila, lime juice, orange liqueur, ancho chile liqueur, and simple syrup if using.

Add Ice: Fill the shaker with ice cubes.

Shake Vigorously: Shake well until the shaker becomes frosty and cold, about 15-20 seconds.

Strain: Strain the cocktail into the prepared glass filled with fresh ice.

Garnish: Place a lime wedge on the rim of the glass.

Serve: Serve immediately and enjoy the spicy and smoky flavors of your Ancho Chile Margarita.

Apple Cinnamon Margarita

- 2 oz tequila
- 1 oz apple cider
- 1/2 oz triple sec
- 1/2 oz lime juice, freshly squeezed
- 1/4 oz cinnamon syrup (or simple syrup with a pinch of ground cinnamon)
- Ice cubes
- Cinnamon sugar for rimming the glass
- Apple slice and a cinnamon stick for garnish

Prepare the Rim: Mix some cinnamon with sugar. Rub a lime wedge around the rim of a margarita glass and dip it into the cinnamon sugar mixture.

Combine Ingredients: In a cocktail shaker, combine the tequila, apple cider, triple sec, lime juice, and cinnamon syrup.

Add Ice: Fill the shaker with ice cubes.

Shake Vigorously: Shake well until the mixture is thoroughly chilled.

Strain: Strain the cocktail into the prepared glass filled with fresh ice.

Garnish: Decorate with an apple slice and a cinnamon stick.

Serve: Serve immediately and enjoy the warm, spicy flavors of your Apple Cinnamon Margarita.

Apple Spice Margarita

- ➤ **2 oz tequila**
- ➤ **1 oz apple cider**
- ➤ **1/2 oz triple sec**
- ➤ **1/2 oz lime juice, freshly squeezed**
- ➤ **1 cup water**
- ➤ **1 cup granulated sugar**
- ➤ **2 cinnamon sticks**
- ➤ **1 teaspoon ground nutmeg**
- ➤ **1/2 teaspoon ground cloves**
- ➤ **Ice cubes**
- ➤ **Cinnamon and sugar for rimming the glass**
- ➤ **Apple slice and a sprinkle of ground nutmeg for garnish**

Make Spiced Syrup: In a small saucepan, combine water, sugar, cinnamon sticks, nutmeg, and cloves. Bring to a boil, then reduce heat and simmer for about 10 minutes. Allow to cool, then strain out the solids.

Prepare the Rim: Mix cinnamon with sugar. Rub a lime wedge around the rim of a margarita glass and dip it into the cinnamon sugar mixture.

Combine Ingredients: In a cocktail shaker, combine the tequila, apple cider, triple sec, lime juice, and cooled spiced syrup.

Add Ice: Fill the shaker with ice cubes.

Shake Vigorously: Shake well until the mixture is thoroughly chilled.

Strain: Strain the cocktail into the prepared glass filled with fresh ice.

Garnish: Decorate with an apple slice and a sprinkle of ground nutmeg.

Serve: Serve immediately and enjoy the warm, spiced flavors of your Apple Spice Margarita.

Apricot Margarita

- 2 oz tequila
- 1 oz apricot puree
  - 3-4 ripe apricots, pitted and diced
- 1/2 oz lime juice, freshly squeezed
- 1/2 oz triple sec
- 1/2 oz simple syrup
- Ice cubes
- Salt or sugar for rimming the glass
- Apricot slice and lime wheel for garnish

Make Apricot Puree: Blend the diced apricots until smooth. Strain through a fine mesh sieve to remove any pulp if desired.

Prepare the Rim: Rub a lime wedge around the rim of a margarita glass and dip it into salt or sugar.

Combine Ingredients: In a cocktail shaker, combine the tequila, apricot puree, lime juice, triple sec, and simple syrup.

Add Ice: Fill the shaker with ice cubes.

Shake Vigorously: Shake well until the mixture is thoroughly chilled.

Strain: Strain the cocktail into the prepared glass filled with fresh ice.

Garnish: Decorate with an apricot slice and a lime wheel.

Serve: Serve immediately and enjoy the sweet and fruity flavors of your Apricot Margarita.

Avocado Margarita

- 2 oz tequila
- 1/2 ripe avocado, peeled and pitted
- 1 oz lime juice, freshly squeezed
- 1/2 oz triple sec
- 1/2 oz simple syrup
- Ice cubes
- Salt for rimming the glass
- Lime wedge for garnish

Prepare the Avocado: Scoop the avocado flesh into a blender.

Combine Ingredients: Add the tequila, lime juice, triple sec, and simple syrup to the blender.

Blend: Blend until the mixture is smooth.

Prepare the Rim: Rub a lime wedge around the rim of a margarita glass and dip it into salt.

Add Ice to Glass: Fill the glass with ice cubes.

Pour: Pour the blended mixture over the ice in the glass.

Garnish: Decorate with a lime wedge.

Serve: Serve immediately and enjoy the creamy and refreshing flavors of your Avocado Margarita.

Balsamic Margarita

- 2 oz tequila
- 1 oz lime juice, freshly squeezed
- 1/2 oz triple sec
- 1/2 oz balsamic vinegar
- 1/2 oz agave syrup or simple syrup
- Ice cubes
- Salt and cracked black pepper for rimming the glass
- Lime wheel for garnish

Prepare the Rim: Mix salt and a little cracked black pepper. Rub a lime wedge around the rim of a margarita glass and dip it into the salt-pepper mixture.

Combine Ingredients: In a cocktail shaker, combine the tequila, lime juice, triple sec, balsamic vinegar, and agave syrup.

Add Ice: Fill the shaker with ice cubes.

Shake Vigorously: Shake well until the mixture is thoroughly chilled.

Strain: Strain the cocktail into the prepared glass filled with fresh ice.

Garnish: Decorate with a lime wheel.

Serve: Serve immediately and savor the complex and layered flavors of your Balsamic Margarita.

Banana Margarita

- 2 oz tequila
- I ripe banana, peeled
- I oz lime juice, freshly squeezed
- 1/2 oz triple sec
- 1/2 oz simple syrup
- Ice cubes
- Salt for rimming the glass
- Lime wedge and a slice of banana for garnish

Prepare the Banana: Slice the banana into smaller pieces for easier blending.

Combine Ingredients: In a blender, combine the tequila, banana pieces, lime juice, triple sec, and simple syrup.

Blend: Blend until smooth.

Prepare the Rim: Rub a lime wedge around the rim of a margarita glass and dip it into salt.

Add Ice to Glass: Fill the glass with ice cubes.

Pour: Pour the blended mixture over the ice in the glass.

Garnish: Decorate with a lime wedge and a slice of banana.

Serve: Serve immediately and enjoy the smooth, fruity flavors of your Banana Margarita.

Basil Watermelon Margarita

- 2 oz tequila
- 1 oz watermelon juice, freshly extracted
- 1/2 oz lime juice, freshly squeezed
- 1/2 oz simple syrup
- 3-4 fresh basil leaves, plus extra for garnish
- Ice cubes
- Salt for rimming the glass
- Small watermelon slice and a basil leaf for garnish

Prepare Watermelon Juice: If not already done, blend fresh watermelon in a blender until smooth, then strain through a fine mesh sieve to remove seeds and pulp.

Muddle Basil: In a cocktail shaker, gently muddle the basil leaves with the simple syrup to release their aromatic oils.

Combine Ingredients: Add the watermelon juice, lime juice, and tequila to the shaker.

Add Ice: Fill the shaker with ice cubes.

Shake Vigorously: Shake well until the mixture is thoroughly chilled.

Strain: Strain the cocktail into a chilled glass rimmed with salt.

Garnish: Decorate with a small slice of watermelon and a basil leaf.

Serve: Serve immediately and enjoy the refreshing, herbaceous flavors of your Basil Watermelon Margarita.

Berry Trio Margarita

- 2 oz tequila
- 1/2 oz triple sec
- 1/2 oz lime juice, freshly squeezed
- 1/4 cup mixed berries (such as strawberries, raspberries, and blueberries)
- 1/2 oz simple syrup
- Ice cubes
- Salt for rimming the glass
- Fresh berries for garnish

Muddle Berries: In a cocktail shaker, muddle the mixed berries with the simple syrup to release their juices.

Combine Ingredients: Add the tequila, triple sec, and lime juice to the shaker.

Add Ice: Fill the shaker with ice cubes.

Shake Vigorously: Shake well until the mixture is thoroughly chilled.

Strain: Strain the cocktail into a chilled glass rimmed with salt. You can double strain to ensure a smoother texture without seeds.

Garnish: Decorate with a skewer of fresh berries.

Serve: Serve immediately and enjoy the fresh, fruity flavors of your Berry Trio Margarita.

Black Currant Margarita

- 2 oz tequila
- 1 oz black currant puree or juice
  - 1 cup fresh or frozen black currants
  - 1-2 tablespoons water
- 1/2 oz lime juice, freshly squeezed
- 1/2 oz triple sec
- 1/2 oz simple syrup
- Ice cubes
- Salt or sugar for rimming the glass
- Lime wheel and black currants for garnish

Make Black Currant Puree: Blend the black currants with a small amount of water until smooth. Strain through a fine mesh sieve to remove any pulp and seeds.

Prepare the Rim: Rub a lime wedge around the rim of a margarita glass and dip it into salt or sugar.

Combine Ingredients: In a cocktail shaker, combine the tequila, black currant puree or juice, lime juice, triple sec, and simple syrup.

Add Ice: Fill the shaker with ice cubes.

Shake Vigorously: Shake well until the mixture is thoroughly chilled.

Strain: Strain the cocktail into the prepared glass filled with fresh ice.

Garnish: Decorate with a lime wheel and a few black currants.

Serve: Serve immediately and enjoy the rich and tangy flavors of your Black Currant Margarita.

Blackberry Sage Margarita

- 2 oz tequila
- 1 oz blackberry puree
  - 1 cup fresh blackberries
  - 1-2 tablespoons water
- 1/2 oz lime juice, freshly squeezed
- 1/2 oz triple sec
- 1/2 oz sage-infused simple syrup
  - 1 cup water
  - 1 cup sugar
  - 4-6 fresh sage leaves
- Ice cubes
- Sugar or salt for rimming the glass
- Fresh blackberries and sage leaves for garnish

Make Blackberry Puree: Blend the blackberries with a small amount of water until smooth. Strain through a fine mesh sieve to remove any pulp and seeds.

Prepare the Rim: Rub a lime wedge around the rim of a margarita glass and dip it into sugar or salt.

Combine Ingredients: In a cocktail shaker, combine the tequila, blackberry puree, lime juice, triple sec, and sage-infused simple syrup.

Add Ice: Fill the shaker with ice cubes.

Shake Vigorously: Shake well until the mixture is thoroughly chilled.

Strain: Strain the cocktail into the prepared glass filled with fresh ice.

Garnish: Garnish with fresh blackberries and sage leaves.

Serve: Serve immediately and enjoy the sweet and herbal flavors of your Blackberry Sage Margarita.

Blood Orange Margarita

- 2 oz tequila
- 1 oz blood orange juice, freshly squeezed
- 1/2 oz lime juice, freshly squeezed
- 1/2 oz triple sec
- 1/4 oz simple syrup
- Ice cubes
- Salt for rimming the glass
- Blood orange slice and lime wheel for garnish

Prepare the Rim: Rub a lime wedge around the rim of a margarita glass and dip it into salt.

Combine Ingredients: In a cocktail shaker, combine the tequila, blood orange juice, lime juice, triple sec, and simple syrup if using.

Add Ice: Fill the shaker with ice cubes.

Shake Vigorously: Shake well until the mixture is thoroughly chilled.

Strain: Strain the cocktail into the prepared glass filled with fresh ice.

Garnish: Decorate with a blood orange slice and a lime wheel.

Serve: Serve immediately and enjoy the refreshing and vibrant flavors of your Blood Orange Margarita.

Blue Curacao Margarita

- ➤ *2 oz tequila*
- ➤ *1 oz blue curaçao*
- ➤ *1/2 oz lime juice, freshly squeezed*
- ➤ *1/2 oz simple syrup*
- ➤ *Ice cubes*
- ➤ *Salt for rimming the glass*
- ➤ *Lime wedge and a slice of orange for garnish*

Prepare the Rim: Rub a lime wedge around the rim of a margarita glass and dip it into salt.

Combine Ingredients: In a cocktail shaker, combine the tequila, blue curaçao, lime juice, and simple syrup.

Add Ice: Fill the shaker with ice cubes.

Shake Vigorously: Shake well until the mixture is thoroughly chilled.

Strain: Strain the cocktail into the prepared glass filled with fresh ice.

Garnish: Decorate with a lime wedge and a slice of orange.

Serve: Serve immediately and enjoy the vibrant, tropical flavors of your Blue Curaçao Margarita.

Blueberry Basil Margarita

- ➤ 2 oz tequila
- ➤ 1 oz blueberry puree
  - ○ 1 cup fresh blueberries
  - ○ 1-2 tablespoons water
- ➤ 1/2 oz lime juice, freshly squeezed
- ➤ 1/2 oz triple sec
- ➤ 1/2 oz simple syrup
- ➤ Ice cubes
- ➤ Sugar or salt for rimming the glass
- ➤ Fresh blueberries and basil leaves for garnish

Make Blueberry Puree: Blend the blueberries with a small amount of water until smooth. Strain through a fine mesh sieve to remove any pulp and seeds.

Prepare the Rim: Rub a lime wedge around the rim of a margarita glass and dip it into sugar or salt.

Combine Ingredients: In a cocktail shaker, combine the tequila, blueberry puree, lime juice, triple sec, and simple syrup.

Add Ice: Fill the shaker with ice cubes.

Shake Vigorously: Shake well until the mixture is thoroughly chilled.

Strain: Strain the cocktail into the prepared glass filled with fresh ice.

Garnish: Garnish with fresh blueberries and basil leaves.

Serve: Serve immediately and enjoy the sweet and herbal flavors of your Blueberry Basil Margarita.

Cantaloupe Margarita

- ➤ 2 oz tequila
- ➤ 1 oz cantaloupe puree
  - ○ 1 cup diced cantaloupe
- ➤ 1/2 oz lime juice, freshly squeezed
- ➤ 1/2 oz triple sec
- ➤ 1/2 oz simple syrup
- ➤ Ice cubes
- ➤ Salt or sugar for rimming the glass
- ➤ Cantaloupe slice and lime wheel for garnish

Make Cantaloupe Puree: Blend the diced cantaloupe until smooth. Strain through a fine mesh sieve to remove any pulp.

Prepare the Rim: Rub a lime wedge around the rim of a margarita glass and dip it into salt or sugar.

Combine Ingredients: In a cocktail shaker, combine the tequila, cantaloupe puree, lime juice, triple sec, and simple syrup.

Add Ice: Fill the shaker with ice cubes.

Shake Vigorously: Shake well until the mixture is thoroughly chilled.

Strain: Strain the cocktail into the prepared glass filled with fresh ice.

Garnish: Decorate with a cantaloupe slice and a lime wheel.

Serve: Serve immediately and enjoy the sweet and refreshing flavors of your Cantaloupe Margarita.

Caramel Apple Margarita

- ➤ 2 oz tequila
- ➤ 1 oz apple cider
- ➤ 1/2 oz triple sec
- ➤ 1/2 oz lime juice, freshly squeezed
- ➤ 1/2 oz caramel syrup
- ➤ Ice cubes
- ➤ Cinnamon and sugar for rimming the glass
- ➤ Apple slice and a drizzle of caramel for garnish

Make Caramel Syrup: (if making homemade) In a small saucepan, combine 1 cup sugar and 1/4 cup water. Heat over medium-high, stirring until the sugar dissolves and turns a deep amber color. Remove from heat and carefully stir in 1/2 cup heavy cream. Allow to cool before using.

Prepare the Rim: Mix cinnamon with sugar. Rub a lime wedge around the rim of a margarita glass and dip it into the cinnamon sugar mixture.

Combine Ingredients: In a cocktail shaker, combine the tequila, apple cider, triple sec, lime juice, and caramel syrup.

Add Ice: Fill the shaker with ice cubes.

Shake Vigorously: Shake well until the mixture is thoroughly chilled.

Strain: Strain the cocktail into the prepared glass filled with fresh ice.

Garnish: Decorate with an apple slice and a drizzle of caramel over the top.

Serve: Serve immediately and enjoy the rich, sweet flavors of your Caramel Apple Margarita.

Caramelized Banana Margarita

- 2 oz tequila
- 1/2 oz triple sec
- 1 oz lime juice, freshly squeezed
- 1/2 oz simple syrup
- 1 ripe banana
- 1 tbsp brown sugar
- 1 tsp butter
- Ice cubes
- Salt or sugar for rimming the glass
- Banana slice for garnish

Caramelize the Banana: In a small pan, melt the butter over medium heat. Add the brown sugar and stir until it starts to melt. Slice the banana and add the slices to the pan. Cook until the banana slices are caramelized, about 2-3 minutes on each side. Allow to cool.

Blend Ingredients: In a blender, combine the caramelized banana slices, tequila, triple sec, lime juice, and simple syrup. Blend until smooth.

Prepare the Rim: Rub a lime wedge around the rim of a margarita glass and dip it into salt or sugar.

Add Ice: Fill the prepared glass with ice cubes.

Pour: Pour the blended mixture over the ice in the glass.

Garnish: Decorate with a banana slice.

Serve: Serve immediately and enjoy the rich, creamy flavors of your Caramelized Banana Margarita.

Cardamom Margarita

- 2 oz tequila
- 1 oz lime juice, freshly squeezed
- 1/2 oz triple sec
- 1/2 oz simple syrup
- 1/4 tsp ground cardamom
- Ice cubes
- Salt or sugar for rimming the glass
- Lime wheel and a sprinkle of ground cardamom for garnish

Prepare the Rim: Rub a lime wedge around the rim of a margarita glass and dip it into salt or sugar.

Infuse Cardamom: If using cardamom pods, gently crush them to release the seeds, and mix with the simple syrup in a small saucepan. Heat gently for a few minutes (do not boil), then let cool and strain. If using ground cardamom, simply mix it directly into the simple syrup.

Combine Ingredients: In a cocktail shaker, combine the tequila, lime juice, triple sec, and cardamom-infused simple syrup (or syrup with ground cardamom).

Add Ice: Fill the shaker with ice cubes.

Shake Vigorously: Shake well until the mixture is thoroughly chilled.

Strain: Strain the cocktail into the prepared glass filled with fresh ice.

Garnish: Decorate with a lime wheel and a sprinkle of ground cardamom.

Serve: Serve immediately and enjoy the exotic and aromatic flavors of your Cardamom Margarita.

Carrot Margarita

- 2 oz tequila
- 1 oz fresh carrot juice
  - 2-3 large carrots, washed and peeled
- 1/2 oz lime juice, freshly squeezed
- 1/2 oz triple sec
- 1/2 oz simple syrup
- Ice cubes
- Salt for rimming the glass
- Carrot twist and lime wheel for garnish

Make Carrot Juice: Juice the carrots using a juicer. If you don't have a juicer, blend the carrots with a small amount of water and strain through a fine mesh sieve to extract the juice.

Prepare the Rim: Rub a lime wedge around the rim of a margarita glass and dip it into salt.

Combine Ingredients: In a cocktail shaker, combine the tequila, fresh carrot juice, lime juice, triple sec, and simple syrup.

Add Ice: Fill the shaker with ice cubes.

Shake Vigorously: Shake well until the mixture is thoroughly chilled.

Strain: Strain the cocktail into the prepared glass filled with fresh ice.

Garnish: Decorate with a carrot twist and a lime wheel.

Serve: Serve immediately and enjoy the fresh and vibrant flavors of your Carrot Margarita.

Chamomile Margarita

- 2 oz tequila
- 1 oz chamomile tea syrup
  - 1 cup water
  - 1 cup sugar
  - 2-3 chamomile tea bags
- 1/2 oz lime juice, freshly squeezed
- 1/2 oz triple sec
- Ice cubes
- Salt or sugar for rimming the glass
- Lime wheel and chamomile flowers for garnish

Make Chamomile Tea Syrup: In a small saucepan, bring water and sugar to a boil. Remove from heat, add chamomile tea bags, and let steep for 10-15 minutes. Remove the tea bags and allow the syrup to cool.

Prepare the Rim: Rub a lime wedge around the rim of a margarita glass and dip it into salt or sugar.

Combine Ingredients: In a cocktail shaker, combine the tequila, chamomile tea syrup, lime juice, and triple sec.

Add Ice: Fill the shaker with ice cubes.

Shake Vigorously: Shake well until the mixture is thoroughly chilled.

Strain: Strain the cocktail into the prepared glass filled with fresh ice.

Garnish: Decorate with a lime wheel and chamomile flowers if available.

Serve: Serve immediately and enjoy the calming and refreshing flavors of your Chamomile Margarita.

Cherry Lime Margarita

- 2 oz tequila
- 1 oz fresh cherry puree
  - 1 cup fresh or frozen cherries, pitted
- 1/2 oz lime juice, freshly squeezed
- 1/2 oz triple sec
- 1/2 oz simple syrup
- Ice cubes
- Salt or sugar for rimming the glass
- Fresh cherries and lime wheel for garnish

Make Cherry Puree: Blend the pitted cherries until smooth. Strain through a fine mesh sieve to remove any pulp.

Prepare the Rim: Rub a lime wedge around the rim of a margarita glass and dip it into salt or sugar.

Combine Ingredients: In a cocktail shaker, combine the tequila, cherry puree, lime juice, triple sec, and simple syrup.

Add Ice: Fill the shaker with ice cubes.

Shake Vigorously: Shake well until the mixture is thoroughly chilled.

Strain: Strain the cocktail into the prepared glass filled with fresh ice.

Garnish: Decorate with fresh cherries and a lime wheel.

Serve: Serve immediately and enjoy the sweet and tangy flavors of your Cherry Lime Margarita.

Chili Lime Margarita

- 2 oz tequila
- 1 oz lime juice, freshly squeezed
- 1/2 oz triple sec
- 1/2 oz simple syrup
- 1 slice of fresh jalapeño
- Ice cubes
- Tajín or chili powder and salt for rimming the glass
- Lime wheel and a slice of chili for garnish

Prepare the Rim: Mix Tajín or chili powder with salt. Rub a lime wedge around the rim of a margarita glass and dip it into the chili-salt mixture.

Muddle Chili: In a cocktail shaker, gently muddle the jalapeño or chili slice with the simple syrup to release the heat.

Combine Ingredients: Add the tequila, lime juice, and triple sec to the shaker.

Add Ice: Fill the shaker with ice cubes.

Shake Vigorously: Shake well until the mixture is thoroughly chilled.

Strain: Strain the cocktail into the prepared glass filled with fresh ice.

Garnish: Decorate with a lime wheel and a slice of chili.

Serve: Serve immediately and enjoy the spicy and tangy flavors of your Chili Lime Margarita.

Chocolate Orange Margarita

- *2 oz tequila*
- *1 oz triple sec*
- *1 oz orange juice, freshly squeezed*
- *1/2 oz lime juice, freshly squeezed*
- *1/2 oz chocolate syrup*
- *Ice cubes*
- *Cocoa powder and sugar for rimming the glass*
- *Orange twist and a piece of chocolate for garnish*

Prepare the Rim: Mix cocoa powder with sugar. Rub an orange wedge around the rim of a margarita glass and dip it into the cocoa-sugar mixture.

Combine Ingredients: In a cocktail shaker, combine the tequila, triple sec, orange juice, lime juice, and chocolate syrup.

Add Ice: Fill the shaker with ice cubes.

Shake Vigorously: Shake well until the mixture is thoroughly chilled.

Strain: Strain the cocktail into the prepared glass filled with fresh ice.

Garnish: Decorate with an orange twist and a piece of chocolate.

Serve: Serve immediately and enjoy the rich, citrusy flavors of your Chocolate Orange Margarita.

Clove and Orange Margarita

- 2 oz tequila
- 1 oz fresh orange juice
- 1/2 oz lime juice, freshly squeezed
- 1/2 oz triple sec
- 1/2 oz clove-infused simple syrup
  - 1 cup water
  - 1 cup sugar
  - 1 tbsp whole cloves
- Ice cubes
- Salt or sugar for rimming the glass
- Orange slice and a sprinkle of ground cloves for garnish

Make Clove-Infused Simple Syrup: In a small saucepan, combine water, sugar, and whole cloves. Bring to a boil, then reduce heat and simmer for about 10 minutes. Allow to cool, then strain out the cloves. Store the syrup in a sealed container in the refrigerator.

Prepare the Rim: Rub an orange wedge around the rim of a margarita glass and dip it into salt or sugar.

Combine Ingredients: In a cocktail shaker, combine the tequila, fresh orange juice, lime juice, triple sec, and clove-infused simple syrup.

Add Ice: Fill the shaker with ice cubes.

Shake Vigorously: Shake well until the mixture is thoroughly chilled.

Strain: Strain the cocktail into the prepared glass filled with fresh ice.

Garnish: Decorate with an orange slice and a sprinkle of ground cloves.

Serve: Serve immediately and enjoy the spicy and citrusy flavors of your Clove and Orange Margarita.

Coconut Lime Margarita

- 2 oz tequila
- 1 oz coconut cream (or coconut milk for a lighter version)
- 1 oz lime juice, freshly squeezed
- 1/2 oz triple sec
- 1/2 oz simple syrup
- Ice cubes
- Toasted coconut flakes for rimming the glass
- Lime wheel and a sprinkle of toasted coconut for garnish

Prepare the Rim: Toast some coconut flakes in a dry pan until golden brown. Let them cool. Rub a lime wedge around the rim of a margarita glass and dip it into the toasted coconut flakes.

Combine Ingredients: In a cocktail shaker, combine the tequila, coconut cream, lime juice, triple sec, and simple syrup.

Add Ice: Fill the shaker with ice cubes.

Shake Vigorously: Shake well until the mixture is thoroughly chilled.

Strain: Strain the cocktail into the prepared glass filled with fresh ice.

Garnish: Decorate with a lime wheel and a sprinkle of toasted coconut.

Serve: Serve immediately and enjoy the tropical and refreshing flavors of your Coconut Lime Margarita.

Cranberry Margarita

- 2 oz tequila
- 1 oz cranberry juice
- 1/2 oz triple sec
- 1/2 oz lime juice, freshly squeezed
- 1/2 oz simple syrup
- Ice cubes
- Salt or sugar for rimming the glass
- Fresh cranberries and a lime wheel for garnish

Prepare the Rim: Rub a lime wedge around the rim of a margarita glass and dip it into salt or sugar.

Combine Ingredients: In a cocktail shaker, combine the tequila, cranberry juice, triple sec, lime juice, and simple syrup if using.

Add Ice: Fill the shaker with ice cubes.

Shake Vigorously: Shake well until the mixture is thoroughly chilled.

Strain: Strain the cocktail into the prepared glass filled with fresh ice.

Garnish: Decorate with fresh cranberries and a lime wheel.

Serve: Serve immediately and enjoy the tart and fruity flavors of your Cranberry Margarita.

Cucumber Mint Margarita

- ➤ *2 oz tequila*
- ➤ *1 oz lime juice, freshly squeezed*
- ➤ *1/2 oz triple sec*
- ➤ *1/2 oz simple syrup*
- ➤ *4-5 slices of cucumber, plus extra for garnish*
- ➤ *4-5 fresh mint leaves, plus extra for garnish*
- ➤ *Ice cubes*
- ➤ *Salt for rimming the glass*

Muddle Cucumber and Mint: In a cocktail shaker, gently muddle the cucumber slices and mint leaves with the simple syrup to release their flavors.

Combine Ingredients: Add the tequila, lime juice, and triple sec to the shaker.

Add Ice: Fill the shaker with ice cubes.

Shake Vigorously: Shake well until the mixture is thoroughly chilled.

Prepare the Rim: Rub a lime wedge around the rim of a margarita glass and dip it into salt.

Strain: Strain the cocktail into the prepared glass filled with fresh ice.

Garnish: Decorate with extra cucumber slices and a sprig of mint.

Serve: Serve immediately and enjoy the cool, refreshing flavors of your Cucumber Mint Margarita.

Cucumber Watermelon Margarita

- 2 oz tequila
- 1 oz fresh watermelon juice
  - 1 cup diced watermelon
- 1 oz cucumber juice
  - 1 medium cucumber, peeled and chopped
- 1/2 oz lime juice, freshly squeezed
- 1/2 oz triple sec
- 1/2 oz simple syrup
- Ice cubes
- Salt or sugar for rimming the glass
- Watermelon slice and cucumber ribbon for garnish

Make Watermelon Juice: Blend the diced watermelon until smooth. Strain through a fine mesh sieve to remove any pulp and seeds.

Make Cucumber Juice: Blend the chopped cucumber until smooth. Strain through a fine mesh sieve to remove any pulp.

Prepare the Rim: Rub a lime wedge around the rim of a margarita glass and dip it into salt or sugar.

Combine Ingredients: In a cocktail shaker, combine the tequila, watermelon juice, cucumber juice, lime juice, triple sec, and simple syrup.

Add Ice: Fill the shaker with ice cubes.

Shake Vigorously: Shake well until the mixture is thoroughly chilled.

Strain: Strain the cocktail into the prepared glass filled with fresh ice.

Garnish: Decorate with a watermelon slice and a ribbon of cucumber.

Serve: Serve immediately and enjoy the refreshing flavors of your Cucumber Watermelon Margarita.

Dragon Fruit Margarita

- 2 oz tequila
- 1 oz dragon fruit puree
  - 1 dragon fruit, peeled and diced
- 1/2 oz lime juice, freshly squeezed
- 1/2 oz triple sec
- 1/2 oz simple syrup
- Ice cubes
- Salt or sugar for rimming the glass
- Lime wheel and dragon fruit slice for garnish

Make Dragon Fruit Puree: Blend the diced dragon fruit until smooth. Strain through a fine mesh sieve to remove any seeds if desired.

Prepare the Rim: Rub a lime wedge around the rim of a margarita glass and dip it into salt or sugar.

Combine Ingredients: In a cocktail shaker, combine the tequila, dragon fruit puree, lime juice, triple sec, and simple syrup.

Add Ice: Fill the shaker with ice cubes.

Shake Vigorously: Shake well until the mixture is thoroughly chilled.

Strain: Strain the cocktail into the prepared glass filled with fresh ice.

Garnish: Decorate with a lime wheel and a slice of dragon fruit on the rim.

Serve: Serve immediately and enjoy the vibrant and refreshing flavors of your Dragon Fruit Margarita.

Espresso Margarita

- 2 oz tequila
- 1 oz freshly brewed espresso (cooled)
- 1/2 oz coffee liqueur
- 1/2 oz triple sec
- 1/2 oz simple syrup
- Ice cubes
- Cocoa powder or coffee grounds for rimming the glass
- Coffee beans for garnish

Prepare the Rim: Rub a lime wedge around the rim of a margarita glass and dip it into cocoa powder or coffee grounds.

Combine Ingredients: In a cocktail shaker, combine the tequila, cooled espresso, coffee liqueur, triple sec, and simple syrup.

Add Ice: Fill the shaker with ice cubes.

Shake Vigorously: Shake well until the mixture is thoroughly chilled.

Strain: Strain the cocktail into the prepared glass filled with fresh ice.

Garnish: Decorate with a few coffee beans.

Serve: Serve immediately and enjoy the rich, coffee-infused flavors of your Espresso Margarita.

Fig and Honey Margarita

- ➤ *2 oz tequila*
- ➤ *1 oz fresh fig puree*
  - ○ *4-5 fresh figs, stems removed*
  - ○ *1-2 tablespoons water*
- ➤ *1/2 oz lime juice, freshly squeezed*
- ➤ *1/2 oz triple sec*
- ➤ *1/2 oz honey syrup*
  - ○ *1/2 cup honey*
  - ○ *1/2 cup water*
- ➤ *Ice cubes*
- ➤ *Salt or sugar for rimming the glass*
- ➤ *Fig slice and lime wheel for garnish*

Make Fig Puree: In a blender, combine the fresh figs and water. Blend until smooth, adding more water if necessary to achieve a puree consistency.

Make Honey Syrup: In a small saucepan, combine honey and water. Heat over medium, stirring until the honey is dissolved. Allow to cool and store in a sealed container in the refrigerator.

Prepare the Rim: Rub a lime wedge around the rim of a margarita glass and dip it into salt or sugar.

Combine Ingredients: In a cocktail shaker, combine the tequila, fig puree, lime juice, triple sec, and honey syrup.

Add Ice: Fill the shaker with ice cubes.

Shake Vigorously: Shake well until the mixture is thoroughly chilled.

Strain: Strain the cocktail into the prepared glass filled with fresh ice.

Garnish: Decorate with a fig slice and a lime wheel.

Serve: Serve immediately and enjoy the sweet and rich flavors of your Fig and Honey Margarita.

Fig and Walnut Margarita

- 2 oz tequila
- 1 oz fresh fig puree
  - 4-5 fresh figs, stems removed
  - 1-2 tablespoons water
- 1/2 oz lime juice, freshly squeezed
- 1/2 oz triple sec
- 1/2 oz walnut syrup
  - 1/2 cup walnuts, chopped
  - 1 cup water
  - 1 cup sugar
- Ice cubes
- Crushed walnuts and sugar for rimming the glass
- Fig slice and walnut for garnish

Make Fig Puree: In a blender, combine the fresh figs and water. Blend until smooth, adding more water if necessary to achieve a puree consistency.

Make Walnut Syrup: In a small saucepan, combine chopped walnuts, water, and sugar. Bring to a boil, then reduce heat and simmer for about 10 minutes. Allow to cool, then strain out the walnuts. Store the syrup in a sealed container in the refrigerator.

Prepare the Rim: Mix crushed walnuts with sugar. Rub a lime wedge around the rim of a margarita glass and dip it into the walnut-sugar mixture.

Combine Ingredients: In a cocktail shaker, combine the tequila, fig puree, lime juice, triple sec, and walnut syrup.

Add Ice: Fill the shaker with ice cubes.

Shake Vigorously: Shake well until the mixture is thoroughly chilled.

Strain: Strain the cocktail into the prepared glass filled with fresh ice.

Garnish: Decorate with a fig slice and a walnut.

Serve: Serve immediately and enjoy the rich, nutty, and sweet flavors of your Fig and Walnut Margarita.

Fig Vanilla Margarita

- **2 oz tequila**
- **1 oz fresh fig puree**
  - 4-5 fresh figs, stems removed
  - 1-2 tablespoons water
- **1/2 oz lime juice, freshly squeezed**
- **1/2 oz triple sec**
- **1/2 oz vanilla syrup**
  - 1 cup water
  - 1 cup sugar
  - 1 vanilla bean, split and seeds scraped
- **Ice cubes**
- **Sugar for rimming the glass**
- **Fig slice and vanilla bean for garnish**

Make Fig Puree: In a blender, combine the fresh figs and water. Blend until smooth, adding more water if necessary to achieve a puree consistency.

Make Vanilla Syrup: In a small saucepan, combine water, sugar, and the split vanilla bean with seeds. Bring to a boil, then reduce heat and simmer for about 10 minutes. Allow to cool and remove the vanilla bean. Store the syrup in a sealed container in the refrigerator.

Prepare the Rim: Rub a lime wedge around the rim of a margarita glass and dip it into sugar.

Combine Ingredients: In a cocktail shaker, combine the tequila, fig puree, lime juice, triple sec, and vanilla syrup.

Add Ice: Fill the shaker with ice cubes.

Shake Vigorously: Shake well until the mixture is thoroughly chilled.

Strain: Strain the cocktail into the prepared glass filled with fresh ice.

Garnish: Decorate with a fig slice and a piece of vanilla bean.

Serve: Serve immediately and enjoy the rich, sweet, and smooth flavors of your Fig Vanilla Margarita.

Ginger Margarita

- 2 oz tequila
- 1/2 oz lime juice, freshly squeezed
- 1/2 oz triple sec
- 1/2 oz simple syrup (recipe below)
- 2 oz ginger beer
- Ice cubes
- Salt for rimming the glass
- Lime wheel and a slice of fresh ginger for garnish

Prepare the Rim: Rub a lime wedge around the rim of a margarita glass and dip it into salt.

Combine Ingredients: In a cocktail shaker, combine the tequila, lime juice, triple sec, and simple syrup.

Add Ice: Fill the shaker with ice cubes.

Shake Vigorously: Shake well until the mixture is thoroughly chilled.

Strain: Strain the cocktail into the prepared glass filled with fresh ice.

Top with Ginger Beer: Pour the ginger beer over the top of the strained mixture.

Garnish: Decorate with a lime wheel and a slice of fresh ginger.

Serve: Serve immediately and enjoy the spicy and refreshing flavors of your Ginger Margarita.

Grape Margarita

- 2 oz tequila
- I oz fresh grape juice
- 1/2 oz lime juice, freshly squeezed
- 1/2 oz triple sec
- 1/2 oz simple syrup (recipe below)
- Ice cubes
- Salt or sugar for rimming the glass
- Fresh grapes and a lime wheel for garnish

Prepare the Rim: Rub a lime wedge around the rim of a margarita glass and dip it into salt or sugar.

Combine Ingredients: In a cocktail shaker, combine the tequila, fresh grape juice, lime juice, triple sec, and simple syrup.

Add Ice: Fill the shaker with ice cubes.

Shake Vigorously: Shake well until the mixture is thoroughly chilled.

Strain: Strain the cocktail into the prepared glass filled with fresh ice.

Garnish: Decorate with fresh grapes and a lime wheel.

Serve: Serve immediately and enjoy the refreshing and fruity flavors of your Grape Margarita.

Grapefruit Elderflower Margarita

- ➤ 2 oz tequila
- ➤ 1 oz fresh grapefruit juice
- ➤ 1/2 oz lime juice, freshly squeezed
- ➤ 1/2 oz elderflower liqueur
- ➤ 1/2 oz simple syrup
- ➤ Ice cubes
- ➤ Salt or sugar for rimming the glass
- ➤ Grapefruit slice and a sprig of fresh mint for garnish

Prepare the Rim: Rub a grapefruit wedge around the rim of a margarita glass and dip it into salt or sugar.

Combine Ingredients: In a cocktail shaker, combine the tequila, fresh grapefruit juice, lime juice, elderflower liqueur, and simple syrup.

Add Ice: Fill the shaker with ice cubes.

Shake Vigorously: Shake well until the mixture is thoroughly chilled.

Strain: Strain the cocktail into the prepared glass filled with fresh ice.

Garnish: Decorate with a grapefruit slice and a sprig of fresh mint.

Serve: Serve immediately and enjoy the tart, floral flavors of your Grapefruit Elderflower Margarita.

Green Tea Margarita

- 2 oz tequila
- 1 oz brewed green tea, cooled
- 1/2 oz lime juice, freshly squeezed
- 1/2 oz triple sec
- 1/2 oz simple syrup
- Ice cubes
- Salt for rimming the glass
- Lime wheel and mint leaves for garnish

Prepare the Rim: Rub a lime wedge around the rim of a margarita glass and dip it into salt.

Combine Ingredients: In a cocktail shaker, combine the tequila, brewed green tea, lime juice, triple sec, and simple syrup.

Add Ice: Fill the shaker with ice cubes.

Shake Vigorously: Shake well until the mixture is thoroughly chilled.

Strain: Strain the cocktail into the prepared glass filled with fresh ice.

Garnish: Decorate with a lime wheel and mint leaves.

Serve: Serve immediately and enjoy the refreshing and earthy flavors of your Green Tea Margarita.

Hibiscus Margarita

- ➤ 2 oz tequila
- ➤ 1 oz hibiscus tea, cooled
- ➤ 1/2 oz lime juice, freshly squeezed
- ➤ 1/2 oz triple sec
- ➤ 1/2 oz simple syrup
- ➤ Ice cubes
- ➤ Salt or sugar for rimming the glass
- ➤ Lime wheel and hibiscus flower for garnish

Prepare the Rim: Rub a lime wedge around the rim of a margarita glass and dip it into salt or sugar.

Combine Ingredients: In a cocktail shaker, combine the tequila, hibiscus tea, lime juice, triple sec, and simple syrup.

Add Ice: Fill the shaker with ice cubes.

Shake Vigorously: Shake well until the mixture is thoroughly chilled.

Strain: Strain the cocktail into the prepared glass filled with fresh ice.

Garnish: Decorate with a lime wheel and a hibiscus flower, if available.

Serve: Serve immediately and enjoy the tart and floral flavors of your Hibiscus Margarita.

Honey Lemon Margarita

- ➤ **2 oz tequila**
- ➤ **1 oz lemon juice, freshly squeezed**
- ➤ **1/2 oz triple sec**
- ➤ **1/2 oz honey syrup**
  - ○ **1/2 cup honey**
  - ○ **1/2 cup water**
- ➤ **Ice cubes**
- ➤ **Salt or sugar for rimming the glass**
- ➤ **Lemon wheel and a drizzle of honey for garnish**

Make Honey Syrup: In a small saucepan, combine honey and water. Heat over medium, stirring until the honey is dissolved. Allow to cool and store in a sealed container in the refrigerator.

Prepare the Rim: Rub a lemon wedge around the rim of a margarita glass and dip it into salt or sugar.

Combine Ingredients: In a cocktail shaker, combine the tequila, lemon juice, triple sec, and honey syrup.

Add Ice: Fill the shaker with ice cubes.

Shake Vigorously: Shake well until the mixture is thoroughly chilled.

Strain: Strain the cocktail into the prepared glass filled with fresh ice.

Garnish: Decorate with a lemon wheel and a drizzle of honey.

Serve: Serve immediately and enjoy the sweet and tart flavors of your Honey Lemon Margarita.

Honeydew Margarita

- 2 oz tequila
- 1 oz honeydew melon puree
  - 1 cup diced honeydew melon
- 1/2 oz lime juice, freshly squeezed
- 1/2 oz triple sec
- 1/2 oz simple syrup
- Ice cubes
- Salt or sugar for rimming the glass
- Honeydew melon slice and lime wheel for garnish

Make Honeydew Melon Puree: Blend the diced honeydew melon until smooth. Strain through a fine mesh sieve to remove any pulp if desired.

Prepare the Rim: Rub a lime wedge around the rim of a margarita glass and dip it into salt or sugar.

Combine Ingredients: In a cocktail shaker, combine the tequila, honeydew melon puree, lime juice, triple sec, and simple syrup.

Add Ice: Fill the shaker with ice cubes.

Shake Vigorously: Shake well until the mixture is thoroughly chilled.

Strain: Strain the cocktail into the prepared glass filled with fresh ice.

Garnish: Decorate with a honeydew melon slice and a lime wheel.

Serve: Serve immediately and enjoy the refreshing and fruity flavors of your Honeydew Margarita.

Hot Chocolate Margarita

- ➤ 2 oz tequila
- ➤ I oz triple sec
- ➤ I cup hot chocolate
  - ○ I cup milk
  - ○ 2 tbsp cocoa powder
  - ○ 2 tbsp sugar
  - ○ 1/2 tsp vanilla extract
  - ○ A pinch of salt
- ➤ 1/2 oz simple syrup
- ➤ Ice cubes (optional, for a chilled version)
- ➤ Whipped cream and chocolate shavings for garnish
- ➤ Cocoa powder or sugar for rimming the glass

Make Hot Chocolate: In a small saucepan, combine the milk, cocoa powder, sugar, vanilla extract, and salt. Heat over medium, whisking until the cocoa and sugar are fully dissolved and the mixture is hot.

Prepare the Rim: Rub a lime wedge around the rim of a glass and dip it into cocoa powder or sugar.

Combine Ingredients: In a cocktail shaker or mixing glass, combine the tequila, triple sec, hot chocolate, and simple syrup. For a chilled version, add ice cubes.

Mix Well: Stir well to combine, or shake if using ice.

Strain or Pour: For the chilled version, strain the cocktail into the prepared glass filled with fresh ice. For the hot version, pour directly into the glass.

Garnish: Top with whipped cream and chocolate shavings.

Serve: Serve immediately and enjoy the rich, chocolatey flavors of your Hot Chocolate Margarita.

Kiwi Margarita

- ➤ **2 oz tequila**
- ➤ **1 oz fresh kiwi puree**
  - ○ **2 ripe kiwis, peeled and chopped**
- ➤ **1/2 oz lime juice, freshly squeezed**
- ➤ **1/2 oz triple sec**
- ➤ **1/2 oz simple syrup**
- ➤ **Ice cubes**
- ➤ **Salt or sugar for rimming the glass**
- ➤ **Kiwi slice and lime wheel for garnish**

Make Kiwi Puree: Blend the chopped kiwis until smooth. Strain through a fine mesh sieve to remove any seeds if desired.

Prepare the Rim: Rub a lime wedge around the rim of a margarita glass and dip it into salt or sugar.

Combine Ingredients: In a cocktail shaker, combine the tequila, fresh kiwi puree, lime juice, triple sec, and simple syrup.

Add Ice: Fill the shaker with ice cubes.

Shake Vigorously: Shake well until the mixture is thoroughly chilled.

Strain: Strain the cocktail into the prepared glass filled with fresh ice.

Garnish: Decorate with a kiwi slice and a lime wheel.

Serve: Serve immediately and enjoy the refreshing and fruity flavors of your Kiwi Margarita.

Kiwi Strawberry Margarita

- 2 oz tequila
- 1/2 oz lime juice, freshly squeezed
- 1/2 oz triple sec
- 1 oz simple syrup
- 1/2 cup fresh kiwi puree
  - 2 ripe kiwis, peeled and chopped
- 1/2 cup fresh strawberry puree
  - 1/2 cup fresh strawberries, hulled
- Ice cubes
- Salt or sugar for rimming the glass
- Kiwi slice and strawberry for garnish

Make Kiwi Puree: Blend the chopped kiwis until smooth. Strain through a fine mesh sieve to remove any seeds if desired.

Make Strawberry Puree: Blend the hulled strawberries until smooth. Strain through a fine mesh sieve to remove any seeds if desired.

Prepare the Rim: Rub a lime wedge around the rim of a margarita glass and dip it into salt or sugar.

Combine Ingredients: In a cocktail shaker, combine the tequila, lime juice, triple sec, simple syrup, kiwi puree, and strawberry puree.

Add Ice: Fill the shaker with ice cubes.

Shake Vigorously: Shake well until the mixture is thoroughly chilled.

Strain: Strain the cocktail into the prepared glass filled with fresh ice.

Garnish: Decorate with a kiwi slice and a strawberry.

Serve: Serve immediately and enjoy the refreshing and fruity flavors of your Kiwi Strawberry Margarita.

Lavender Margarita

- 2 oz tequila
- I oz fresh lime juice
- 1/2 oz triple sec
- 1/2 oz lavender syrup
  - I cup water
  - I cup sugar
  - 2 tablespoons dried lavender buds
- Ice cubes
- Salt or sugar for rimming the glass
- Lime wheel and a sprig of lavender for garnish

Make Lavender Syrup: In a small saucepan, combine water, sugar, and dried lavender buds. Bring to a boil, then reduce heat and simmer for about IO minutes. Allow to cool and strain out the lavender buds. Store the syrup in a sealed container in the refrigerator.

Prepare the Rim: Rub a lime wedge around the rim of a margarita glass and dip it into salt or sugar.

Combine Ingredients: In a cocktail shaker, combine the tequila, fresh lime juice, triple sec, and lavender syrup.

Add Ice: Fill the shaker with ice cubes.

Shake Vigorously: Shake well until the mixture is thoroughly chilled.

Strain: Strain the cocktail into the prepared glass filled with fresh ice.

Garnish: Decorate with a lime wheel and a sprig of lavender.

Serve: Serve immediately and enjoy the aromatic and refreshing flavors of your Lavender Margarita.

Lemon Basil Margarita

- 2 oz tequila
- 1 oz fresh lemon juice
- 1/2 oz triple sec
- 1/2 oz simple syrup
- 4-5 fresh basil leaves, plus extra for garnish
- Ice cubes
- Salt or sugar for rimming the glass
- Lemon wheel and basil sprig for garnish

Muddle Basil: In a cocktail shaker, gently muddle the fresh basil leaves with the simple syrup to release their aromatic oils.

Combine Ingredients: Add the tequila, fresh lemon juice, and triple sec to the shaker.

Add Ice: Fill the shaker with ice cubes.

Shake Vigorously: Shake well until the mixture is thoroughly chilled.

Prepare the Rim: Rub a lemon wedge around the rim of a margarita glass and dip it into salt or sugar.

Strain: Strain the cocktail into the prepared glass filled with fresh ice.

Garnish: Decorate with a lemon wheel and a sprig of basil.

Serve: Serve immediately and enjoy the zesty and refreshing flavors of your Lemon Basil Margarita.

Lemon Ginger Margarita

- ➤ 2 oz tequila
- ➤ 1 oz fresh lemon juice
- ➤ 1/2 oz triple sec
- ➤ 1/2 oz ginger syrup
  - ○ 1/2 cup water
  - ○ 1/2 cup sugar
  - ○ 1/4 cup fresh ginger, peeled and sliced
- ➤ Ice cubes
- ➤ Salt or sugar for rimming the glass
- ➤ Lemon wheel and fresh ginger slice for garnish

Make Ginger Syrup: In a small saucepan, combine water, sugar, and fresh ginger slices. Bring to a boil, then reduce heat and simmer for about 10 minutes. Allow to cool and strain out the ginger slices. Store the syrup in a sealed container in the refrigerator.

Prepare the Rim: Rub a lemon wedge around the rim of a margarita glass and dip it into salt or sugar.

Combine Ingredients: In a cocktail shaker, combine the tequila, fresh lemon juice, triple sec, and ginger syrup.

Add Ice: Fill the shaker with ice cubes.

Shake Vigorously: Shake well until the mixture is thoroughly chilled.

Strain: Strain the cocktail into the prepared glass filled with fresh ice.

Garnish: Decorate with a lemon wheel and a slice of fresh ginger.

Serve: Serve immediately and enjoy the zesty and spicy flavors of your Lemon Ginger Margarita.

Lemonade Margarita

- ➤ 2 oz tequila
- ➤ 2 oz lemonade
- ➤ 1/2 oz lime juice, freshly squeezed
- ➤ 1/2 oz triple sec
- ➤ 1/2 oz simple syrup
- ➤ Ice cubes
- ➤ Salt or sugar for rimming the glass
- ➤ Lemon wheel and lime wheel for garnish

Prepare the Rim: Rub a lemon wedge around the rim of a margarita glass and dip it into salt or sugar.

Combine Ingredients: In a cocktail shaker, combine the tequila, lemonade, lime juice, triple sec, and simple syrup.

Add Ice: Fill the shaker with ice cubes.

Shake Vigorously: Shake well until the mixture is thoroughly chilled.

Strain: Strain the cocktail into the prepared glass filled with fresh ice.

Garnish: Decorate with a lemon wheel and a lime wheel.

Serve: Serve immediately and enjoy the refreshing and tart flavors of your Lemonade Margarita.

Lychee Margarita

- 2 oz tequila
- 1 oz lychee juice (from canned lychees or fresh lychees blended and strained)
- 1/2 oz lime juice, freshly squeezed
- 1/2 oz triple sec
- 1/2 oz simple syrup
- Ice cubes
- Salt or sugar for rimming the glass
- Lychee fruit and lime wheel for garnish

Prepare the Rim: Rub a lime wedge around the rim of a margarita glass and dip it into salt or sugar.

Combine Ingredients: In a cocktail shaker, combine the tequila, lychee juice, lime juice, triple sec, and simple syrup.

Add Ice: Fill the shaker with ice cubes.

Shake Vigorously: Shake well until the mixture is thoroughly chilled.

Strain: Strain the cocktail into the prepared glass filled with fresh ice.

Garnish: Decorate with a lychee fruit and a lime wheel.

Serve: Serve immediately and enjoy the sweet and exotic flavors of your Lychee Margarita.

Maple Bacon Margarita

- ➤ **2 oz bacon-infused tequila**
  - ○ *4 slices of cooked bacon*
  - ○ *1 cup tequila*
- ➤ *1 oz lime juice, freshly squeezed*
- ➤ *1/2 oz triple sec*
- ➤ *1/2 oz maple syrup*
- ➤ *Ice cubes*
- ➤ *Salt or sugar for rimming the glass*
- ➤ *Crispy bacon strip and lime wheel for garnish*

Make Bacon-Infused Tequila: In a jar, combine the cooked bacon and tequila. Let it infuse for at least 24 hours, or overnight for a stronger flavor. Strain the tequila through a fine mesh sieve or cheesecloth to remove the bacon pieces.

Prepare the Rim: Rub a lime wedge around the rim of a margarita glass and dip it into salt or sugar.

Combine Ingredients: In a cocktail shaker, combine the bacon-infused tequila, lime juice, triple sec, and maple syrup.

Add Ice: Fill the shaker with ice cubes.

Shake Vigorously: Shake well until the mixture is thoroughly chilled.

Strain: Strain the cocktail into the prepared glass filled with fresh ice.

Garnish: Decorate with a crispy bacon strip and a lime wheel.

Serve: Serve immediately and enjoy the smoky, sweet, and savory flavors of your Maple Bacon Margarita.

Matcha Margarita

- ➤ 2 oz tequila
- ➤ 1 oz lime juice, freshly squeezed
- ➤ 1/2 oz triple sec
- ➤ 1/2 oz agave syrup
- ➤ 1/2 teaspoon matcha powder
- ➤ Ice cubes
- ➤ Salt or sugar for rimming the glass
- ➤ Lime wheel and a sprinkle of matcha powder for garnish

Prepare the Rim: Rub a lime wedge around the rim of a margarita glass and dip it into salt or sugar.

Mix Matcha: In a small bowl, whisk the matcha powder with a small amount of hot water until smooth. Let it cool slightly.

Combine Ingredients: In a cocktail shaker, combine the tequila, lime juice, triple sec, agave syrup, and the matcha mixture. Shake well to mix thoroughly.

Add Ice: Fill the shaker with ice cubes.

Shake Vigorously: Shake well until the mixture is thoroughly chilled.

Strain: Strain the cocktail into the prepared glass filled with fresh ice.

Garnish: Decorate with a lime wheel and a sprinkle of matcha powder.

Serve: Serve immediately and enjoy the unique and refreshing flavors of your Matcha Margarita.

Miso Margarita

- 2 oz tequila
- 1 oz lime juice, freshly squeezed
- 1/2 oz triple sec
- 1/2 oz simple syrup
- 1/2 teaspoon white miso paste
- Ice cubes
- Salt for rimming the glass
- Lime wheel for garnish

Prepare the Rim: Rub a lime wedge around the rim of a margarita glass and dip it into salt.

Mix Miso: In a small bowl, whisk the miso paste with a small amount of water until smooth and fully dissolved.

Combine Ingredients: In a cocktail shaker, combine the tequila, lime juice, triple sec, simple syrup, and miso mixture. Shake well to mix thoroughly.

Add Ice: Fill the shaker with ice cubes.

Shake Vigorously: Shake well until the mixture is thoroughly chilled.

Strain: Strain the cocktail into the prepared glass filled with fresh ice.

Garnish: Decorate with a lime wheel.

Serve: Serve immediately and enjoy the unique and savory flavors of your Miso Margarita.

Mojito Margarita

- 2 oz tequila
- 1 oz lime juice, freshly squeezed
- 1/2 oz triple sec
- 1/2 oz simple syrup
- 4-5 fresh mint leaves, plus extra for garnish
- 1 oz club soda
- Ice cubes
- Salt or sugar for rimming the glass
- Lime wheel and mint sprig for garnish

Prepare the Rim: Rub a lime wedge around the rim of a margarita glass and dip it into salt or sugar.

Muddle Mint: In a cocktail shaker, gently muddle the fresh mint leaves with the simple syrup to release their aromatic oils.

Combine Ingredients: Add the tequila, lime juice, and triple sec to the shaker.

Add Ice: Fill the shaker with ice cubes.

Shake Vigorously: Shake well until the mixture is thoroughly chilled.

Strain: Strain the cocktail into the prepared glass filled with fresh ice.

Add Club Soda: Top off the drink with club soda.

Garnish: Decorate with a lime wheel and a sprig of mint.

Serve: Serve immediately and enjoy the refreshing combination of mojito and margarita flavors in your Mojito Margarita.

Orange Blossom Margarita

- 2 oz tequila
- 1 oz fresh orange juice
- 1/2 oz lime juice, freshly squeezed
- 1/2 oz triple sec
- 1/4 oz simple syrup
- 1/4 oz orange blossom water
- Ice cubes
- Salt or sugar for rimming the glass
- Orange wheel and edible flowers for garnish

Prepare the Rim: Rub an orange wedge around the rim of a margarita glass and dip it into salt or sugar.

Combine Ingredients: In a cocktail shaker, combine the tequila, fresh orange juice, lime juice, triple sec, simple syrup, and orange blossom water.

Add Ice: Fill the shaker with ice cubes.

Shake Vigorously: Shake well until the mixture is thoroughly chilled.

Strain: Strain the cocktail into the prepared glass filled with fresh ice.

Garnish: Decorate with an orange wheel and edible flowers if desired.

Serve: Serve immediately and enjoy the fragrant and refreshing flavors of your Orange Blossom Margarita.

Orange Ginger Margarita

- 2 oz tequila
- 1 oz fresh orange juice
- 1/2 oz lime juice, freshly squeezed
- 1/2 oz triple sec
- 1/2 oz ginger syrup
  - 1/2 cup water
  - 1/2 cup sugar
  - 1/4 cup fresh ginger, peeled and sliced
- Ice cubes
- Salt or sugar for rimming the glass
- Orange wheel and a slice of fresh ginger for garnish

Make Ginger Syrup: In a small saucepan, combine water, sugar, and fresh ginger slices. Bring to a boil, then reduce heat and simmer for about 10 minutes. Allow to cool and strain out the ginger slices. Store the syrup in a sealed container in the refrigerator.

Prepare the Rim: Rub an orange wedge around the rim of a margarita glass and dip it into salt or sugar.

Combine Ingredients: In a cocktail shaker, combine the tequila, fresh orange juice, lime juice, triple sec, and ginger syrup.

Add Ice: Fill the shaker with ice cubes.

Shake Vigorously: Shake well until the mixture is thoroughly chilled.

Strain: Strain the cocktail into the prepared glass filled with fresh ice.

Garnish: Decorate with an orange wheel and a slice of fresh ginger.

Serve: Serve immediately and enjoy the zesty and spicy flavors of your Orange Ginger Margarita.

Orange Marmalade Margarita

- 2 oz tequila
- 1 oz lime juice, freshly squeezed
- 1/2 oz triple sec
- 1/2 oz simple syrup
- 1 tablespoon orange marmalade
- Ice cubes
- Salt or sugar for rimming the glass
- Orange wheel and lime wheel for garnish

Prepare the Rim: Rub an orange wedge around the rim of a margarita glass and dip it into salt or sugar.

Combine Ingredients: In a cocktail shaker, combine the tequila, lime juice, triple sec, simple syrup, and orange marmalade. Stir well to ensure the marmalade is fully dissolved.

Add Ice: Fill the shaker with ice cubes.

Shake Vigorously: Shake well until the mixture is thoroughly chilled.

Strain: Strain the cocktail into the prepared glass filled with fresh ice.

Garnish: Decorate with an orange wheel and a lime wheel.

Serve: Serve immediately and enjoy the tangy and sweet flavors of your Orange Marmalade Margarita.

Passion Fruit Margarita

- ➤ 2 oz tequila
- ➤ 1 oz passion fruit puree or juice
  - ○ 2-3 ripe passion fruits
- ➤ 1/2 oz lime juice, freshly squeezed
- ➤ 1/2 oz triple sec
- ➤ 1/2 oz simple syrup
- ➤ Ice cubes
- ➤ Salt or sugar for rimming the glass
- ➤ Lime wheel and passion fruit slice for garnish

Make Passion Fruit Puree/Juice: Cut the passion fruits in half and scoop out the pulp. Blend the pulp briefly to separate the juice from the seeds, then strain to remove the seeds.

Prepare the Rim: Rub a lime wedge around the rim of a margarita glass and dip it into salt or sugar.

Combine Ingredients: In a cocktail shaker, combine the tequila, passion fruit puree or juice, lime juice, triple sec, and simple syrup.

Add Ice: Fill the shaker with ice cubes.

Shake Vigorously: Shake well until the mixture is thoroughly chilled.

Strain: Strain the cocktail into the prepared glass filled with fresh ice.

Garnish: Decorate with a lime wheel and a passion fruit slice.

Serve: Serve immediately and enjoy the tangy and tropical flavors of your Passion Fruit Margarita.

Peach Thyme Margarita

- 2 oz tequila
- 1 oz fresh peach puree
  - 1 ripe peach, peeled, pitted, and diced
- 1/2 oz lime juice, freshly squeezed
- 1/2 oz triple sec
- 1/2 oz thyme syrup
  - 1/2 cup water
  - 1/2 cup sugar
  - 5-6 fresh thyme sprigs
- Ice cubes
- Salt or sugar for rimming the glass
- Peach slice and thyme sprig for garnish

Make Peach Puree: Blend the diced peach until smooth. Strain through a fine mesh sieve to remove any pulp if desired.

Make Thyme Syrup: In a small saucepan, combine water, sugar, and fresh thyme sprigs. Bring to a boil, then reduce heat and simmer for about 10 minutes. Allow to cool and strain out the thyme sprigs. Store the syrup in a sealed container in the refrigerator.

Prepare the Rim: Rub a lime wedge around the rim of a margarita glass and dip it into salt or sugar.

Combine Ingredients: In a cocktail shaker, combine the tequila, peach puree, lime juice, triple sec, and thyme syrup.

Add Ice: Fill the shaker with ice cubes.

Shake Vigorously: Shake well until the mixture is thoroughly chilled.

Strain: Strain the cocktail into the prepared glass filled with fresh ice.

Garnish: Decorate with a peach slice and a sprig of thyme.

Serve: Serve immediately and enjoy the sweet and herbal flavors of your Peach Thyme Margarita.

Pear Ginger Margarita

- ➤ 2 oz tequila
- ➤ 1 oz fresh pear puree
  - ○ 1 ripe pear, peeled, cored, and diced
- ➤ 1/2 oz lime juice, freshly squeezed
- ➤ 1/2 oz triple sec
- ➤ 1/2 oz ginger syrup
  - ○ 1/2 cup water
  - ○ 1/2 cup sugar
  - ○ 1/4 cup fresh ginger, peeled and sliced
- ➤ Ice cubes
- ➤ Salt or sugar for rimming the glass
- ➤ Pear slice and ginger slice for garnish

Make Pear Puree: Blend the diced pear until smooth. Strain through a fine mesh sieve to remove any pulp if desired.

Make Ginger Syrup: In a small saucepan, combine water, sugar, and fresh ginger slices. Bring to a boil, then reduce heat and simmer for about 10 minutes. Allow to cool and strain out the ginger slices. Store the syrup in a sealed container in the refrigerator.

Prepare the Rim: Rub a lime wedge around the rim of a margarita glass and dip it into salt or sugar.

Combine Ingredients: In a cocktail shaker, combine the tequila, pear puree, lime juice, triple sec, and ginger syrup.

Add Ice: Fill the shaker with ice cubes.

Shake Vigorously: Shake well until the mixture is thoroughly chilled.

Strain: Strain the cocktail into the prepared glass filled with fresh ice.

Garnish: Decorate with a pear slice and a slice of fresh ginger.

Serve: Serve immediately and enjoy the sweet and spicy flavors of your Pear Ginger Margarita.

Peppermint Margarita

- 2 oz tequila
- 1 oz lime juice, freshly squeezed
- 1/2 oz triple sec
- 1/2 oz peppermint syrup
  - 1/2 cup water
  - 1/2 cup sugar
  - 1 teaspoon peppermint extract
- Ice cubes
- Crushed candy canes or sugar for rimming the glass
- Mint leaves and a small candy cane for garnish

Make Peppermint Syrup: In a small saucepan, combine water and sugar. Heat over medium, stirring until the sugar is dissolved. Remove from heat and stir in the peppermint extract. Allow to cool and store in a sealed container in the refrigerator.

Prepare the Rim: Crush some candy canes and mix with sugar. Rub a lime wedge around the rim of a margarita glass and dip it into the crushed candy cane mixture.

Combine Ingredients: In a cocktail shaker, combine the tequila, lime juice, triple sec, and peppermint syrup.

Add Ice: Fill the shaker with ice cubes.

Shake Vigorously: Shake well until the mixture is thoroughly chilled.

Strain: Strain the cocktail into the prepared glass filled with fresh ice.

Garnish: Decorate with fresh mint leaves and a small candy cane.

Serve: Serve immediately and enjoy the festive and refreshing flavors of your Peppermint Margarita.

Pineapple Cilantro Margarita

- 2 oz tequila
- 1 oz fresh pineapple juice
- 1/2 oz lime juice, freshly squeezed
- 1/2 oz triple sec
- 1/2 oz simple syrup
- 4-5 fresh cilantro leaves, plus extra for garnish
- Ice cubes
- Salt or sugar for rimming the glass
- Pineapple wedge and cilantro sprig for garnish

Muddle Cilantro: In a cocktail shaker, gently muddle the fresh cilantro leaves with the simple syrup to release their aromatic oils.

Combine Ingredients: Add the tequila, fresh pineapple juice, lime juice, and triple sec to the shaker.

Add Ice: Fill the shaker with ice cubes.

Shake Vigorously: Shake well until the mixture is thoroughly chilled.

Prepare the Rim: Rub a lime wedge around the rim of a margarita glass and dip it into salt or sugar.

Strain: Strain the cocktail into the prepared glass filled with fresh ice.

Garnish: Decorate with a pineapple wedge and a sprig of cilantro.

Serve: Serve immediately and enjoy the tropical and refreshing flavors of your Pineapple Cilantro Margarita.

Pink Peppercorn Margarita

- 2 oz tequila
- 1 oz lime juice, freshly squeezed
- 1/2 oz triple sec
- 1/2 oz simple syrup
- 1/4 tsp pink peppercorns, crushed
- Ice cubes
- Salt or sugar for rimming the glass
- Lime wheel and a few whole pink peppercorns for garnish

Crush Pink Peppercorns: Using a mortar and pestle or a spice grinder, crush the pink peppercorns to release their aroma.

Combine Ingredients: In a cocktail shaker, combine the tequila, lime juice, triple sec, simple syrup, and crushed pink peppercorns.

Add Ice: Fill the shaker with ice cubes.

Shake Vigorously: Shake well until the mixture is thoroughly chilled.

Prepare the Rim: Rub a lime wedge around the rim of a margarita glass and dip it into salt or sugar.

Strain: Strain the cocktail into the prepared glass filled with fresh ice, ensuring the pink peppercorn bits are strained out.

Garnish: Decorate with a lime wheel and a few whole pink peppercorns.

Serve: Serve immediately and enjoy the sophisticated and subtly spicy flavors of your Pink Peppercorn Margarita.

Pistachio Margarita

- 2 oz tequila
- 1 oz lime juice, freshly squeezed
- 1/2 oz triple sec
- 1/2 oz pistachio syrup
  - 1/2 cup shelled pistachios
  - 1 cup water
  - 1 cup sugar
- 1/2 oz simple syrup
- Ice cubes
- Salt or sugar for rimming the glass
- Crushed pistachios and lime wheel for garnish

Make Pistachio Syrup: In a small saucepan, combine the water and sugar. Bring to a boil, then reduce heat and add the shelled pistachios. Simmer for about 10 minutes. Allow to cool, then blend the mixture until smooth and strain to remove any solids. Store the syrup in a sealed container in the refrigerator.

Prepare the Rim: Rub a lime wedge around the rim of a margarita glass and dip it into salt or sugar, then into crushed pistachios.

Combine Ingredients: In a cocktail shaker, combine the tequila, lime juice, triple sec, pistachio syrup, and simple syrup.

Add Ice: Fill the shaker with ice cubes.

Shake Vigorously: Shake well until the mixture is thoroughly chilled.

Strain: Strain the cocktail into the prepared glass filled with fresh ice.

Garnish: Decorate with a lime wheel and a sprinkle of crushed pistachios.

Serve: Serve immediately and enjoy the creamy, nutty flavors of your Pistachio Margarita.

Pomegranate Margarita

- ➤ 2 oz tequila
- ➤ 1 oz pomegranate juice
- ➤ 1/2 oz lime juice, freshly squeezed
- ➤ 1/2 oz triple sec
- ➤ 1/2 oz simple syrup
- ➤ Ice cubes
- ➤ Salt or sugar for rimming the glass
- ➤ Pomegranate seeds and lime wheel for garnish

Prepare the Rim: Rub a lime wedge around the rim of a margarita glass and dip it into salt or sugar.

Combine Ingredients: In a cocktail shaker, combine the tequila, pomegranate juice, lime juice, triple sec, and simple syrup.

Add Ice: Fill the shaker with ice cubes.

Shake Vigorously: Shake well until the mixture is thoroughly chilled.

Strain: Strain the cocktail into the prepared glass filled with fresh ice.

Garnish: Decorate with a few pomegranate seeds and a lime wheel.

Serve: Serve immediately and enjoy the tart and refreshing flavors of your Pomegranate Margarita.

Prickly Pear Margarita

- 2 oz tequila
- 1 oz fresh prickly pear puree
  - 1-2 prickly pears, peeled and diced
- 1/2 oz lime juice, freshly squeezed
- 1/2 oz triple sec
- 1/2 oz simple syrup
- Ice cubes
- Salt or sugar for rimming the glass
- Lime wheel and prickly pear slice for garnish

Make Prickly Pear Puree: Blend the peeled and diced prickly pears until smooth. Strain through a fine mesh sieve to remove any seeds.

Prepare the Rim: Rub a lime wedge around the rim of a margarita glass and dip it into salt or sugar.

Combine Ingredients: In a cocktail shaker, combine the tequila, prickly pear puree, lime juice, triple sec, and simple syrup.

Add Ice: Fill the shaker with ice cubes.

Shake Vigorously: Shake well until the mixture is thoroughly chilled.

Strain: Strain the cocktail into the prepared glass filled with fresh ice.

Garnish: Decorate with a lime wheel and a slice of prickly pear.

Serve: Serve immediately and enjoy the vibrant and refreshing flavors of your Prickly Pear Margarita.

Pumpkin Spice Margarita

- 2 oz tequila
- 1 oz pumpkin puree
- 1/2 oz lime juice, freshly squeezed
- 1/2 oz triple sec
- 1/2 oz simple syrup
- 1/4 tsp pumpkin pie spice
- Ice cubes
- Cinnamon sugar for rimming the glass
- Cinnamon stick and lime wheel for garnish

Prepare the Rim: Mix cinnamon with sugar. Rub a lime wedge around the rim of a margarita glass and dip it into the cinnamon sugar mixture.

Combine Ingredients: In a cocktail shaker, combine the tequila, pumpkin puree, lime juice, triple sec, simple syrup, and pumpkin pie spice.

Add Ice: Fill the shaker with ice cubes.

Shake Vigorously: Shake well until the mixture is thoroughly chilled and the ingredients are well combined.

Strain: Strain the cocktail into the prepared glass filled with fresh ice.

Garnish: Decorate with a cinnamon stick and a lime wheel.

Serve: Serve immediately and enjoy the warm and spicy flavors of your Pumpkin Spice Margarita.

Raspberry Rosemary Margarita

- 2 oz tequila
- 1 oz fresh raspberry puree
    - 1/2 cup fresh or frozen raspberries
    - 1-2 tablespoons water
- 1/2 oz lime juice, freshly squeezed
- 1/2 oz triple sec
- 1/2 oz simple syrup
- 2-3 fresh rosemary leaves, plus extra for garnish
- Ice cubes
- Salt or sugar for rimming the glass
- Fresh raspberries and rosemary sprig for garnish

Make Raspberry Puree: Blend the raspberries with water until smooth. Strain through a fine mesh sieve to remove the seeds.

Muddle Rosemary: In a cocktail shaker, gently muddle the fresh rosemary leaves with the simple syrup to release their aromatic oils.

Combine Ingredients: Add the tequila, raspberry puree, lime juice, and triple sec to the shaker.

Add Ice: Fill the shaker with ice cubes.

Shake Vigorously: Shake well until the mixture is thoroughly chilled.

Prepare the Rim: Rub a lime wedge around the rim of a margarita glass and dip it into salt or sugar.

Strain: Strain the cocktail into the prepared glass filled with fresh ice.

Garnish: Decorate with fresh raspberries and a sprig of rosemary.

Serve: Serve immediately and enjoy the sweet and herbal flavors of your Raspberry Rosemary Margarita.

Rhubarb Margarita

- 2 oz tequila
- 1 oz fresh rhubarb syrup
  - 1 cup chopped rhubarb
  - 1 cup water
  - 1 cup sugar
- 1/2 oz lime juice, freshly squeezed
- 1/2 oz triple sec
- Ice cubes
- Salt or sugar for rimming the glass
- Lime wheel and a small piece of rhubarb for garnish

Make Rhubarb Syrup: In a small saucepan, combine chopped rhubarb, water, and sugar. Bring to a boil, then reduce heat and simmer for about 10-15 minutes until the rhubarb is soft and the mixture is slightly thickened. Strain through a fine mesh sieve, pressing the solids to extract as much liquid as possible. Allow to cool and store in a sealed container in the refrigerator.

Prepare the Rim: Rub a lime wedge around the rim of a margarita glass and dip it into salt or sugar.

Combine Ingredients: In a cocktail shaker, combine the tequila, rhubarb syrup, lime juice, and triple sec.

Add Ice: Fill the shaker with ice cubes.

Shake Vigorously: Shake well until the mixture is thoroughly chilled.

Strain: Strain the cocktail into the prepared glass filled with fresh ice.

Garnish: Decorate with a lime wheel and a small piece of rhubarb.

Serve: Serve immediately and enjoy the tangy and refreshing flavors of your Rhubarb Margarita.

Rose Margarita

- 2 oz tequila
- 1 oz lime juice, freshly squeezed
- 1/2 oz triple sec
- 1/2 oz rose syrup
  - 1 cup water
  - 1 cup sugar
  - 1/4 cup dried edible rose petals
- Ice cubes
- Salt or sugar for rimming the glass
- Rose petal and lime wheel for garnish

Make Rose Syrup: In a small saucepan, combine water and sugar. Bring to a boil, stirring until the sugar is dissolved. Add dried rose petals the mixture and simmer for 10 minutes. Strain and allow to cool.

Prepare the Rim: Rub a lime wedge around the rim of a margarita glass and dip it into salt or sugar.

Combine Ingredients: In a cocktail shaker, combine the tequila, lime juice, triple sec, and rose syrup.

Add Ice: Fill the shaker with ice cubes.

Shake Vigorously: Shake well until the mixture is thoroughly chilled.

Strain: Strain the cocktail into the prepared glass filled with fresh ice.

Garnish: Decorate with a rose petal and a lime wheel.

Serve: Serve immediately and enjoy the floral and refreshing flavors of your Rose Margarita.

Ruby Red Margarita

- 2 oz tequila
- 1 oz fresh ruby red grapefruit juice
- 1/2 oz lime juice, freshly squeezed
- 1/2 oz triple sec
- 1/2 oz simple syrup
- Ice cubes
- Salt or sugar for rimming the glass
- Grapefruit wedge and lime wheel for garnish

Prepare the Rim: Rub a lime wedge around the rim of a margarita glass and dip it into salt or sugar.

Combine Ingredients: In a cocktail shaker, combine the tequila, fresh ruby red grapefruit juice, lime juice, triple sec, and simple syrup.

Add Ice: Fill the shaker with ice cubes.

Shake Vigorously: Shake well until the mixture is thoroughly chilled.

Strain: Strain the cocktail into the prepared glass filled with fresh ice.

Garnish: Decorate with a grapefruit wedge and a lime wheel.

Serve: Serve immediately and enjoy the sweet and tangy flavors of your Ruby Red Margarita.

Saffron Margarita

- 2 oz tequila
- 1 oz lime juice, freshly squeezed
- 1/2 oz triple sec
- 1/2 oz saffron syrup
  - 1 cup water
  - 1 cup sugar
  - A pinch of saffron threads
- Ice cubes
- Salt or sugar for rimming the glass
- Lime wheel and a few saffron threads for garnish

Make Saffron Syrup: In a small saucepan, combine water and sugar. Bring to a boil, stirring until the sugar is dissolved. Add a pinch of saffron threads and let simmer for 5-10 minutes. Allow to cool and strain out the saffron threads. Store the syrup in a sealed container in the refrigerator.

Prepare the Rim: Rub a lime wedge around the rim of a margarita glass and dip it into salt or sugar.

Combine Ingredients: In a cocktail shaker, combine the tequila, lime juice, triple sec, and saffron syrup.

Add Ice: Fill the shaker with ice cubes.

Shake Vigorously: Shake well until the mixture is thoroughly chilled.

Strain: Strain the cocktail into the prepared glass filled with fresh ice.

Garnish: Decorate with a lime wheel and a few saffron threads.

Serve: Serve immediately and enjoy the exotic and luxurious flavors of your Saffron Margarita.

Sake Margarita

- 2 oz tequila
- 1 oz sake
- 1 oz lime juice, freshly squeezed
- 1/2 oz triple sec
- 1/2 oz simple syrup
- Ice cubes
- Salt for rimming the glass
- Lime wheel and cucumber slice for garnish

Prepare the Rim: Rub a lime wedge around the rim of a margarita glass and dip it into salt.

Combine Ingredients: In a cocktail shaker, combine the tequila, sake, lime juice, triple sec, and simple syrup.

Add Ice: Fill the shaker with ice cubes.

Shake Vigorously: Shake well until the mixture is thoroughly chilled.

Strain: Strain the cocktail into the prepared glass filled with fresh ice.

Garnish: Decorate with a lime wheel and a cucumber slice.

Serve: Serve immediately and enjoy the smooth and refreshing flavors of your Sake Margarita.

Salted Caramel Margarita

- ➤ 2 oz tequila
- ➤ 1 oz lime juice, freshly squeezed
- ➤ 1/2 oz triple sec
- ➤ 1/2 oz salted caramel syrup
- ➤ Ice cubes
- ➤ Salt or crushed pretzels for rimming the glass
- ➤ Caramel sauce for drizzling
- ➤ Lime wheel for garnish

Prepare the Rim: Rub a lime wedge around the rim of a margarita glass and dip it into salt or crushed pretzels.

Combine Ingredients: In a cocktail shaker, combine the tequila, lime juice, triple sec, and salted caramel syrup.

Add Ice: Fill the shaker with ice cubes.

Shake Vigorously: Shake well until the mixture is thoroughly chilled.

Strain: Strain the cocktail into the prepared glass filled with fresh ice.

Drizzle with Caramel: Drizzle caramel sauce inside the glass before pouring the cocktail, if desired.

Garnish: Decorate with a lime wheel.

Serve: Serve immediately and enjoy the rich, sweet, and salty flavors of your Salted Caramel Margarita.

Salted Plum Margarita

- 2 oz tequila
- 1 oz fresh plum puree
  - 2 ripe plums, pitted and chopped
  - 1-2 tablespoons water
- 1/2 oz lime juice, freshly squeezed
- 1/2 oz triple sec
- 1/2 oz simple syrup
- A pinch of sea salt
- Ice cubes
- Salt or sugar for rimming the glass
- Plum slice and lime wheel for garnish

Make Plum Puree: Blend the chopped plums with water until smooth. Strain through a fine mesh sieve to remove any pulp if desired.

Prepare the Rim: Rub a lime wedge around the rim of a margarita glass and dip it into salt or sugar.

Combine Ingredients: In a cocktail shaker, combine the tequila, plum puree, lime juice, triple sec, simple syrup, and a pinch of sea salt.

Add Ice: Fill the shaker with ice cubes.

Shake Vigorously: Shake well until the mixture is thoroughly chilled.

Strain: Strain the cocktail into the prepared glass filled with fresh ice.

Garnish: Decorate with a plum slice and a lime wheel.

Serve: Serve immediately and enjoy the sweet, salty, and tangy flavors of your Salted Plum Margarita.

Smoky Pineapple Margarita

- 2 oz mezcal
- 1 oz fresh pineapple juice
- 1/2 oz lime juice, freshly squeezed
- 1/2 oz triple sec
- 1/2 oz simple syrup
- Ice cubes
- Tajín or smoked salt for rimming the glass
- Pineapple wedge and lime wheel for garnish

Prepare the Rim: Rub a lime wedge around the rim of a margarita glass and dip it into Tajín or smoked salt.

Combine Ingredients: In a cocktail shaker, combine the mezcal, fresh pineapple juice, lime juice, triple sec, and simple syrup.

Add Ice: Fill the shaker with ice cubes.

Shake Vigorously: Shake well until the mixture is thoroughly chilled.

Strain: Strain the cocktail into the prepared glass filled with fresh ice.

Garnish: Decorate with a pineapple wedge and a lime wheel.

Serve: Serve immediately and enjoy the smoky and tropical flavors of your Smoky Pineapple Margarita.

Sour Apple Margarita

- 2 oz tequila
- 1 oz sour apple liqueur
- 1/2 oz lime juice, freshly squeezed
- 1/2 oz triple sec
- 1/2 oz simple syrup
- Ice cubes
- Salt or sugar for rimming the glass
- Apple slice and lime wheel for garnish

Prepare the Rim: Rub a lime wedge around the rim of a margarita glass and dip it into salt or sugar.

Combine Ingredients: In a cocktail shaker, combine the tequila, sour apple liqueur, lime juice, triple sec, and simple syrup.

Add Ice: Fill the shaker with ice cubes.

Shake Vigorously: Shake well until the mixture is thoroughly chilled.

Strain: Strain the cocktail into the prepared glass filled with fresh ice.

Garnish: Decorate with an apple slice and a lime wheel.

Serve: Serve immediately and enjoy the tangy and refreshing flavors of your Sour Apple Margarita.

Sour Cherry Margarita

- ➤ 2 oz tequila
- ➤ 1 oz fresh sour cherry juice
  - ○ 1 cup fresh or frozen sour cherries
  - ○ 1-2 tablespoons water
- ➤ 1/2 oz lime juice, freshly squeezed
- ➤ 1/2 oz triple sec
- ➤ 1/2 oz simple syrup
- ➤ Ice cubes
- ➤ Salt or sugar for rimming the glass
- ➤ Lime wheel and sour cherries for garnish

Make Sour Cherry Juice: Blend the sour cherries with a small amount of water until smooth. Strain through a fine mesh sieve to remove any pulp.

Prepare the Rim: Rub a lime wedge around the rim of a margarita glass and dip it into salt or sugar.

Combine Ingredients: In a cocktail shaker, combine the tequila, sour cherry juice, lime juice, triple sec, and simple syrup.

Add Ice: Fill the shaker with ice cubes.

Shake Vigorously: Shake well until the mixture is thoroughly chilled.

Strain: Strain the cocktail into the prepared glass filled with fresh ice.

Garnish: Decorate with a lime wheel and a few sour cherries.

Serve: Serve immediately and enjoy the tangy and refreshing flavors of your Sour Cherry Margarita.

Spiced Chocolate Margarita

- 2 oz tequila
- 1 oz chocolate liqueur
- 1/2 oz triple sec
- 1/2 oz simple syrup
- 1 oz cream or milk
- 1/4 tsp ground cinnamon
- A pinch of ground cayenne pepper (optional, adjust to taste)
- Ice cubes
- Cocoa powder or cinnamon sugar for rimming the glass
- Chocolate shavings and cinnamon stick for garnish

Prepare the Rim: Mix cocoa powder or cinnamon sugar in a small dish. Rub a lime wedge around the rim of a margarita glass and dip it into the mixture.

Combine Ingredients: In a cocktail shaker, combine the tequila, chocolate liqueur, triple sec, simple syrup, cream or milk, ground cinnamon, and cayenne pepper (if using).

Add Ice: Fill the shaker with ice cubes.

Shake Vigorously: Shake well until the mixture is thoroughly chilled.

Strain: Strain the cocktail into the prepared glass filled with fresh ice.

Garnish: Decorate with chocolate shavings and a cinnamon stick.

Serve: Serve immediately and enjoy the rich, spicy, and chocolatey flavors of your Spiced Chocolate Margarita.

Spiced Pear Margarita

- 2 oz tequila
- 1 oz fresh pear puree
  - 1 ripe pear, peeled, cored, and diced
- 1/2 oz lime juice, freshly squeezed
- 1/2 oz triple sec
- 1/2 oz spiced syrup
  - 1 cup water
  - 1 cup sugar
  - 2 cinnamon sticks
  - 1 teaspoon whole cloves
  - 1/2 teaspoon ground nutmeg
- Ice cubes
- Cinnamon sugar for rimming the glass
- Pear slice and cinnamon stick for garnish

Make Pear Puree: Blend the diced pear until smooth. Strain through a fine mesh sieve to remove any pulp if desired.

Make Spiced Syrup: In a small saucepan, combine water, sugar, cinnamon sticks, whole cloves, and ground nutmeg. Bring to a boil, then reduce heat and simmer for about 10 minutes. Allow to cool and strain out the spices. Store the syrup in a sealed container in the refrigerator.

Prepare the Rim: Mix cinnamon and sugar in a small dish. Rub a lime wedge around the rim of a margarita glass and dip it into the cinnamon sugar mixture.

Combine Ingredients: In a cocktail shaker, combine the tequila, pear puree, lime juice, triple sec, and spiced syrup.

Add Ice: Fill the shaker with ice cubes.

Shake Vigorously: Shake well until the mixture is thoroughly chilled.

Strain: Strain the cocktail into the prepared glass filled with fresh ice.

Garnish: Decorate with a pear slice and a cinnamon stick.

Serve: Serve immediately and enjoy the sweet, spicy, and refreshing flavors of your Spiced Pear Margarita.

Spiced Rum Margarita

- ➤ 2 oz spiced rum
- ➤ 1 oz lime juice, freshly squeezed
- ➤ 1/2 oz triple sec
- ➤ 1/2 oz simple syrup
- ➤ Ice cubes
- ➤ Cinnamon sugar or salt for rimming the glass
- ➤ Lime wheel and cinnamon stick for garnish

Prepare the Rim: Mix cinnamon and sugar (or use salt) in a small dish. Rub a lime wedge around the rim of a margarita glass and dip it into the mixture.

Combine Ingredients: In a cocktail shaker, combine the spiced rum, lime juice, triple sec, and simple syrup.

Add Ice: Fill the shaker with ice cubes.

Shake Vigorously: Shake well until the mixture is thoroughly chilled.

Strain: Strain the cocktail into the prepared glass filled with fresh ice.

Garnish: Decorate with a lime wheel and a cinnamon stick.

Serve: Serve immediately and enjoy the warm and spicy flavors of your Spiced Rum Margarita.

Spicy Mango Margarita

- ➤ 2 oz tequila
- ➤ 1 oz fresh mango puree
  - ○ 1 ripe mango, peeled, pitted, and diced
- ➤ 1/2 oz lime juice, freshly squeezed
- ➤ 1/2 oz triple sec
- ➤ 1/2 oz simple syrup
- ➤ 1-2 slices of fresh jalapeño
- ➤ Ice cubes
- ➤ Tajín or chili powder and salt for rimming the glass
- ➤ Mango slice and jalapeño slice for garnish

Make Mango Puree: Blend the diced mango until smooth. Strain through a fine mesh sieve to remove any pulp if desired.

Prepare the Rim: Mix Tajín or chili powder with salt in a small dish. Rub a lime wedge around the rim of a margarita glass and dip it into the mixture.

Muddle Jalapeño: In a cocktail shaker, gently muddle the fresh jalapeño slices with the simple syrup to release their heat.

Combine Ingredients: Add the tequila, mango puree, lime juice, and triple sec to the shaker.

Add Ice: Fill the shaker with ice cubes.

Shake Vigorously: Shake well until the mixture is thoroughly chilled.

Strain: Strain the cocktail into the prepared glass filled with fresh ice.

Garnish: Decorate with a mango slice and a jalapeño slice.

Serve: Serve immediately and enjoy the sweet and spicy flavors of your Spicy Mango Margarita.

Spicy Melon Margarita

- 2 oz tequila
- 1 oz fresh melon puree
  - 1 cup diced melon
- 1/2 oz lime juice, freshly squeezed
- 1/2 oz triple sec
- 1/2 oz simple syrup
- 1-2 slices of fresh jalapeño
- Ice cubes
- Tajín or chili powder and salt for rimming the glass
- Melon slice and jalapeño slice for garnish

Make Melon Puree: Blend the diced melon until smooth. Strain through a fine mesh sieve to remove any pulp if desired.

Prepare the Rim: Mix Tajín or chili powder with salt in a small dish. Rub a lime wedge around the rim of a margarita glass and dip it into the mixture.

Muddle Jalapeño: In a cocktail shaker, gently muddle the fresh jalapeño slices with the simple syrup to release their heat.

Combine Ingredients: Add the tequila, melon puree, lime juice, and triple sec to the shaker.

Add Ice: Fill the shaker with ice cubes.

Shake Vigorously: Shake well until the mixture is thoroughly chilled.

Strain: Strain the cocktail into the prepared glass filled with fresh ice.

Garnish: Decorate with a melon slice and a jalapeño slice.

Serve: Serve immediately and enjoy the sweet and spicy flavors of your Spicy Melon Margarita.

Starfruit Margarita

- 2 oz tequila
- 1 oz fresh starfruit juice
  - 2-3 ripe starfruits, sliced
- 1/2 oz lime juice, freshly squeezed
- 1/2 oz triple sec
- 1/2 oz simple syrup
- Ice cubes
- Salt or sugar for rimming the glass
- Starfruit slice and lime wheel for garnish

Make Starfruit Juice: Blend the starfruit slices until smooth. Strain through a fine mesh sieve to remove any pulp.

Prepare the Rim: Rub a lime wedge around the rim of a margarita glass and dip it into salt or sugar.

Combine Ingredients: In a cocktail shaker, combine the tequila, starfruit juice, lime juice, triple sec, and simple syrup.

Add Ice: Fill the shaker with ice cubes.

Shake Vigorously: Shake well until the mixture is thoroughly chilled.

Strain: Strain the cocktail into the prepared glass filled with fresh ice.

Garnish: Decorate with a starfruit slice and a lime wheel.

Serve: Serve immediately and enjoy the tangy and refreshing flavors of your Starfruit Margarita.

Strawberry Cucumber Margarita

- ➤ 2 oz tequila
- ➤ 1 oz fresh strawberry puree
    - ○ 1/2 cup fresh strawberries, hulled and sliced
- ➤ 1 oz cucumber juice
    - ○ 1/2 cup peeled and chopped cucumber
- ➤ 1/2 oz lime juice, freshly squeezed
- ➤ 1/2 oz triple sec
- ➤ 1/2 oz simple syrup
- ➤ Ice cubes
- ➤ Salt or sugar for rimming the glass
- ➤ Strawberry slice and cucumber wheel for garnish

Make Strawberry Puree: Blend the strawberries until smooth. Strain through a fine mesh sieve to remove seeds if desired.

Make Cucumber Juice: Blend the chopped cucumber until smooth. Strain through a fine mesh sieve to remove pulp if desired.

Prepare the Rim: Rub a lime wedge around the rim of a margarita glass and dip it into salt or sugar.

Combine Ingredients: In a cocktail shaker, combine the tequila, strawberry puree, cucumber juice, lime juice, triple sec, and simple syrup.

Add Ice: Fill the shaker with ice cubes.

Shake Vigorously: Shake well until the mixture is thoroughly chilled.

Strain: Strain the cocktail into the prepared glass filled with fresh ice.

Garnish: Decorate with a strawberry slice and a cucumber wheel.

Serve: Serve immediately and enjoy the refreshing and unique flavors of your Strawberry Cucumber Margarita.

Tamarind Margarita

- ➤ 2 oz tequila
- ➤ 1 oz tamarind concentrate
  - ○ 1/2 cup tamarind pulp (available in most grocery stores)
  - ○ 1 cup water
- ➤ 1/2 oz lime juice, freshly squeezed
- ➤ 1/2 oz triple sec
- ➤ 1/2 oz simple syrup
- ➤ Ice cubes
- ➤ Tajín or salt for rimming the glass
- ➤ Lime wheel for garnish

Make Tamarind Concentrate: Combine the tamarind pulp and water in a saucepan. Bring to a simmer and cook for about 10 minutes, until the pulp dissolves. Strain through a fine mesh sieve to remove seeds and fibers. Allow to cool.

Prepare the Rim: Rub a lime wedge around the rim of a margarita glass and dip it into Tajín or salt.

Combine Ingredients: In a cocktail shaker, combine the tequila, tamarind concentrate, lime juice, triple sec, and simple syrup.

Add Ice: Fill the shaker with ice cubes.

Shake Vigorously: Shake well until the mixture is thoroughly chilled.

Strain: Strain the cocktail into the prepared glass filled with fresh ice.

Garnish: Decorate with a lime wheel.

Serve: Serve immediately and enjoy the tangy and exotic flavors of your Tamarind Margarita.

Tangerine Margarita

- 2 oz tequila
- 1 oz fresh tangerine puree
  - 2-3 fresh tangerines
- 1/2 oz lime juice, freshly squeezed
- 1/2 oz triple sec
- 1/2 oz simple syrup
- Ice cubes
- Salt or sugar for rimming the glass
- Tangerine slice and lime wheel for garnish

Make Tangerine Puree: Peel the tangerines and remove any seeds. Blend the tangerine segments until smooth. Strain through a fine mesh sieve to remove any pulp if desired.

Prepare the Rim: Rub a tangerine wedge around the rim of a margarita glass and dip it into salt or sugar.

Combine Ingredients: In a cocktail shaker, combine the tequila, fresh tangerine puree, lime juice, triple sec, and simple syrup.

Add Ice: Fill the shaker with ice cubes.

Shake Vigorously: Shake well until the mixture is thoroughly chilled.

Strain: Strain the cocktail into the prepared glass filled with fresh ice.

Garnish: Decorate with a tangerine slice and a lime wheel.

Serve: Serve immediately and enjoy the bright and citrusy flavors of your Tangerine Margarita.

Turmeric Margarita

- 2 oz tequila
- 1 oz lime juice, freshly squeezed
- 1/2 oz triple sec
- 1/2 oz simple syrup
- 1/2 tsp ground turmeric
- A pinch of black pepper (to enhance turmeric absorption)
- Ice cubes
- Salt or sugar for rimming the glass
- Lime wheel and a sprinkle of ground turmeric for garnish

Prepare the Rim: Rub a lime wedge around the rim of a margarita glass and dip it into salt or sugar.

Combine Ingredients: In a cocktail shaker, combine the tequila, lime juice, triple sec, simple syrup, ground turmeric (or fresh turmeric juice), and a pinch of black pepper.

Add Ice: Fill the shaker with ice cubes.

Shake Vigorously: Shake well until the mixture is thoroughly chilled.

Strain: Strain the cocktail into the prepared glass filled with fresh ice.

Garnish: Decorate with a lime wheel and a sprinkle of ground turmeric.

Serve: Serve immediately and enjoy the vibrant and earthy flavors of your Turmeric Margarita.

Vanilla Pear Margarita

- 2 oz tequila
- 1 oz fresh pear puree
  - 1 ripe pear, peeled, cored, and diced
- 1/2 oz lime juice, freshly squeezed
- 1/2 oz triple sec
- 1/2 oz vanilla syrup
  - 1 cup water
  - 1 cup sugar
  - 1 vanilla bean, split and seeds scraped (or 1 tsp vanilla extract)
- Ice cubes
- Sugar for rimming the glass
- Pear slice and vanilla bean for garnish

Make Pear Puree: Blend the diced pear until smooth. Strain through a fine mesh sieve to remove any pulp if desired.

Make Vanilla Syrup: In a small saucepan, combine water and sugar. Add the split vanilla bean and seeds. Bring to a boil, then reduce heat and simmer for about 10 minutes. Remove from heat and allow to cool. If using vanilla extract, add it after removing from heat. Strain out the vanilla bean. Store the syrup in a sealed container in the refrigerator.

Prepare the Rim: Rub a lime wedge around the rim of a margarita glass and dip it into sugar.

Combine Ingredients: In a cocktail shaker, combine the tequila, pear puree, lime juice, triple sec, and vanilla syrup.

Add Ice: Fill the shaker with ice cubes.

Shake Vigorously: Shake well until the mixture is thoroughly chilled.

Strain: Strain the cocktail into the prepared glass filled with fresh ice.

Garnish: Decorate with a pear slice and a piece of vanilla bean.

Serve: Serve immediately and enjoy the sweet and rich flavors of your Vanilla Pear Margarita.

Watermelon Jalapeño Margarita

- 2 oz tequila
- I oz fresh watermelon puree
  - I cup diced watermelon
- 1/2 oz lime juice, freshly squeezed
- 1/2 oz triple sec
- 1/2 oz simple syrup
- 1-2 slices of fresh jalapeño
- Ice cubes
- Tajín or salt for rimming the glass
- Watermelon wedge and jalapeño slice for garnish

Make Watermelon Puree: Blend the diced watermelon until smooth. Strain through a fine mesh sieve to remove any pulp if desired.

Prepare the Rim: Mix Tajín with salt in a small dish. Rub a lime wedge around the rim of a margarita glass and dip it into the Tajín mixture.

Muddle Jalapeño: In a cocktail shaker, gently muddle the fresh jalapeño slices with the simple syrup to release their heat.

Combine Ingredients: Add the tequila, watermelon puree, lime juice, and triple sec to the shaker.

Add Ice: Fill the shaker with ice cubes.

Shake Vigorously: Shake well until the mixture is thoroughly chilled.

Strain: Strain the cocktail into the prepared glass filled with fresh ice.

Garnish: Decorate with a watermelon wedge and a jalapeño slice.

Serve: Serve immediately and enjoy the sweet and spicy flavors of your Watermelon Jalapeño Margarita.

Winter Spice Margarita

- 2 oz tequila
- 1 oz lime juice, freshly squeezed
- 1/2 oz triple sec
- 1/2 oz winter spice syrup
  - 1 cup water
  - 1 cup sugar
  - 2 cinnamon sticks
  - 1 whole star anise
  - 1/2 teaspoon ground nutmeg
- Ice cubes
- Cinnamon sugar for rimming the glass
- Cinnamon stick, star anise, and a sprinkle of nutmeg for garnish

Make Winter Spice Syrup: In a small saucepan, combine water, sugar, cinnamon sticks, star anise, and ground nutmeg. Bring to a boil, then reduce heat and simmer for about 10 minutes. Allow to cool and strain out the spices. Store the syrup in a sealed container in the refrigerator

Prepare the Rim: Mix cinnamon and sugar in a small dish. Rub a lime wedge around the rim of a margarita glass and dip it into the cinnamon sugar mixture.

Combine Ingredients: In a cocktail shaker, combine the tequila, lime juice, triple sec, and winter spice syrup.

Add Ice: Fill the shaker with ice cubes.

Shake Vigorously: Shake well until the mixture is thoroughly chilled.

Strain: Strain the cocktail into the prepared glass filled with fresh ice.

Garnish: Decorate with a cinnamon stick, a star anise, and a sprinkle of nutmeg.

Serve: Serve immediately and enjoy the warm and festive flavors of your Winter Spice Margarita.

Made in the USA
Monee, IL
08 January 2025

75983097R10062